Talkeetna
Good Time

By
Dennis Brown

Copyright © 2008 Dennis Brown
All rights reserved.

ISBN: 1-4196-9347-6
ISBN-13: 9781419693472

Library of Congress Control Number: 2008902424
Visit www.booksurge.com to order additional copies.

Contents

1	Sensation of a Nobody	11
2	Alaska or Bust	31
3	Horse and Sleigh	67
4	Cold	79
5	Dog Boy	89
6	"Bearly" Coffee	101
7	Ill Wind	111
8	Russian Mike	131
9	Mary's Bear	167
10	Gunnysack Gold	181
11	Grandfather	205
12	Don Got My Goat	213
13	Family Car	251

Acknowledgement

My deepest thanks to those who have helped me climb life's mountain. A special thank you to Carol, my loving wife, who has been with me on every adventure and has spent tireless hours editing my work. Thank you, Cory and Les, my two sons, who encouraged me all my life. Family is everything.

I am grateful to Gary Miller and Vic Anderson who assisted with the editing of these stories. I' m also in debt to Dennis Reinke, a talented Estes Park, Colorado artist who painted my "old man" portrait and allowed the painting to be reproduced on the back cover.

Forward

Talkeetna may not be the end of the world, but it is at the end of the road. In 1970, the sign-entering town read; *Welcome to Beautiful Downtown Talkeetna, Population 85.* The sign is still there but the population has changed. What it should say is; *Welcome to Beautiful Downtown Talkeetna. Don't forget to set your watch back 30 years.*

Disclaimer

Contained herein is truth, give or take a lie or two.

Caution

These stories reveal my life in the arctic. Reading these stories may cause some people frostbite.

Dedication

I dedicate these stories to my grandkids. I hope you can accept that your grandfather was a little different. Indeed, I marched to the beat of several different drums. Grandma heard them too.

I want you to remember that money doesn't last very long, friends are hard to find when you are down, and most careers die in a few years. Only family and good memories will last a lifetime.

Sensation of a Nobody

If I could have flown far above my life, I would have seen its wonderful purpose, and perfect plan. I would have realized that I stood on the enormous hand of God.

I don't remember being born, my first birthday, my first Christmas, or my sister's arrival about a year after mine. My first childhood recollection is of Epply Airfield, standing beside my father, watching airplanes come and go. Warm, sunny Sunday afternoons often ended with Pops and me in our 40s model Chevy outside the security fence of the hangar area. We observed the pilots stow their fragile crafts in the T-shaped spaces.

"Daddy what is that?" I said pointing to the orange windsock.

"The pilot puts his plane in there when he's not flying."

"How does he get the airplane in such a tiny thing?"

"The plane is pulled in front, then pushed in backwards."

I didn't ask for more explanation that evening, but never forgot my question. Years later, the answer became apparent. Dad had explained the purpose of a tee hangar, while I asked about the function of a windsock.

My father was a general contractor in Omaha, Nebraska. He preferred quiet, clean, country living, so our home mirrored a gentleman's farm built on a lakeshore. The muddy Elkhorn River flowed only a few hundred feet east of our home. Spring presented the only interruption to the river's continual search for a saltwater rest, when ragged ice flows clogged its southbound travel. The prospect of flooding added excitement and danger to my otherwise peaceful world.

It was my good fortune to attend school at District #22. Cornfields surrounded the one-room white schoolhouse. The bell tower above the front entrance contained a large black bell, which privileged upper classmen rang at the appointed time. My home was about a mile from school; close enough to hear the gong of the bell calling me to take my place. Nine concrete steps ascended from the dirt to the front door; and a small foyer, with a long coatroom on both sides, welcomed the students as they entered.

The boys' and girls' restrooms were located in separate buildings, on opposite sides of the playground, about fifty feet behind the schoolhouse. Painted white, and trimmed in black to match the main structure, these facilities had no running water.

The main classroom was thirty feet by forty feet. The surface of the polished hardwood floor contained one metal grate opening near the center of the room. The coal-burning furnace in the basement provided our only source of heat. During the winter months, it had the ability to slowly transform our frozen ink to a liquid state most days. On the coldest, the entire student body stood on the heat grate until the room's temperature became tolerable. Shivering, and fully bundled with coats and mittens, we attempted our assignments. Good students were appointed seats near the heat. The less favored students sat further away. My assigned seat was far from the heat, so I felt blessed on days when we were allowed to stand on the heated grate.

Two equally spaced light bulbs hung on long cords from the school ceiling. The best students sat closest to the dim light they provided.

Each student was responsible for bringing a thermos containing something to drink, as well as a sack lunch to provide daily nutrition.

One teacher presided over our classroom of thirteen students. Because dyslexia prevented me from reading aloud, I was her least favorite student. This handicap was not understood in the mid 1950s; hence, my label of slow or retarded. I tried my best to please her, but remained a constant irritation to the queen of District #22. Eight years of ridicule and isolation taught me to befriend only myself. I had no classmates in my grade level during my tenure at District #22. The only advantage to this lonely situation was the distinction of graduating number one in my class.

Routine discipline during my grade school years often placed me in a desk facing a corner with my back toward the class. For my inability to read, the teacher endeavored to improve my performance with a leather strap across my butt, or the slap of a yardstick rapped on the back of my knuckles. Sadly, this punishment took place in full view of all the students.

"If you weren't so stupid, Dennis, you would be able to read like the others."

At the time, I accepted my fate, unaware of my inappropriate learning environment. Each year, in spite of an avalanche of D's, she pushed me onto the next grade level. In the fourth grade, I realized I was fortunate in one respect: my near photographic memory compensated for my inability to read aloud. I accepted people's low expectations, and produced only enough to insure passage to the next grade. I often remembered most of the lessons taught to the classes ahead of me. When moved up a grade, I drew upon this reserve of information to answer the questions, often recalling the book and page. Regardless of my instructor's perception, I was convinced of my intelligence, though dyslexia prevented me from proving it. I also realized that I didn't have anything to prove to anyone but myself.

Without my parents' knowledge, I enrolled in college level correspondence courses. Though only fourteen, I scrawled a "21" in the age box on the application. After completing a drafting course and an electronics course, a representative from the University of Nebraska stopped by unannounced to congratulate me on my high marks. He was angry when he discovered my age. Though I had achieved near perfect scores, the university refused any further correspondence courses until I was eighteen years old. No one offered praise for my accomplishment, only ample criticism for lying about my age.

The trek to school through the woods every day was, at times, frightening. In my younger years, the shadows cast by the trees, and the noises of the animals that scurried away into the darkness quickened my pace. In time, however, I learned to feel at home in the forest, and delighted in exploring new places, be it day or night.

It took me the entire summer to save $60 to purchase a Winchester Model 62A, 22-caliber rifle. With my rifle in hand, and my best friend Terry by my side, my days were filled with adventure; we lived off the land and shared good times as only a boy and his dog can. I often returned home famished after living in the woods for three or four days. As I matured and gained experience in the woods, I acquired the skills to survive. By reading Boys' Life and Jack London's books about the north, I perfected my woodsman's skills, residing comfortably for days in the backwoods along the banks of the Elkhorn River. With the discovery of some caves along the banks, winter nights in those hideouts were as comfortable as summer nights under the stars. Always alone, except for Daniel Boone, Davy Crocket, and Jim Bridger, these adventures built up my confidence. The skills I learned served me well in later years.

My graduation from grade school with four other students from country schools took place on May 16, 1959, in Douglas County School District. The Superintendent held a special graduation ceremony to honor the best student from each school. My honor may have been by default, but I earned it.

The next morning, my father directed my energy to assist his paving crew as they poured the concrete for new streets in a nearby subdivision.

"Dad, do I get paid for this work?" I inquired.

"Of course, son. You get one dollar for each hour you work."

"Wow, that's a lot of money!"

"Work hard, son. Spend your money wisely. Someday you'll be an adult. The experience and money you earn will help you in the future. You might even get married someday. That's something to plan for."

The following Friday night, I received my first paycheck. Saturday morning, I walked several miles from my home to a junkyard. The sign above the door of the junkyard shack read, "In God I Trust. Everyone Else Must Pay Cash." A chain, suitable for pulling heavy trucks, restrained the one-eyed bulldog, who ruled the area just short of the entrance.

"Hi, Red. I want to buy that old Model A Ford out back."

"You're not old enough for a car like that. Besides, I want $50 for that beauty. That's a lot of money for a kid. Come back and see me when you get the bucks."

"I've got $29 in my pocket. If you'll fill the tank half full, I'll drive her out of here."

"I won't take a penny less than $50. No offers - $50 and nothing less."

"Maybe I can find a car somewhere else. Thanks for your time, Red." I walked out the door and started for home. I was still within shouting distance when Red called to me.

"Come back here, kid. Don't be in such a big hurry. Show me your money."

I pulled out my paycheck and handed it to Red.

"This ain't no money, it's a check. Can't you read? I deal in cash only."

"My Dad gave me this check, Red. You two know each other. The check is good; you know that."

"Yea, I know him. I guess a check from your Pop's OK. The car's yours. Pick up the title next week."

My trophy was parked near the back of the junkyard. The old bulldog didn't stir when I walked by. Probably ferocious at one time, he now presided there "just for looks."

Sitting behind the wheel, I pulled the hand throttle and spark retard lever several times. The clutch felt normal and allowed me to shift the transmission from gear to gear. The foot throttle and brake functioned as I thought they should. Convinced I could drive my new "wheels," I turned the ignition switch and pressed the starter button. Urrrah, Urrrah, and then nothing.

The battery was dead, but my grandfather had taught me what to do next. I found the hand crank under the seat. *Old man Ford had thought of everything. Let's see...ignition on, gearshift lever in neutral, spark retard lever half way down, and hand throttle down a little.* I slid the hand crank through the small hole located below the radiator and behind the front bumper, locked it in place, and gripped the bar tightly, taking care not to wrap my thumb around the crank handle. Grandfather had taught me well. If the engine kicked back, a thumb could be easily broken. *Thanks, Gramps, for the good advice.*

The compression on the old car was good. It took all my strength to push the crank lever around its path. I cranked away, listening for that "pop" from under the hood. *What had I forgotten? Of course, the choke.* I pulled it full out and cranked again. Pop, pop, pop, and then vroom. She ran!

The drive home along the back roads took longer, but was less risky. If anyone noticed my Ford and me, they never mentioned it. Driving to work was not an option, but the country roads near my home provided me the opportunity to hone my driving skills.

About a month later, while in the barbershop getting my first professional cut, my barber asked. "You know Dave Holland, the Postmaster, don't you? He was in a few days ago for a cut. Did you know his kid got caught speeding on his 'murder' cycle last week? He tried to outrun the State Patrol and lost."

My interest peaked. "Doesn't he live behind the high school? Maybe I should check and see if he's ready to sell his kid's motorcycle. Hey, thanks for the great ducktail cut. I'm making my own money now. I'll be back in a couple weeks."

Mr. Holland's house, a large two-story brick home with a detached two-car garage, was a couple blocks away. The "villain motorcycle" was parked outside in front of the garage, a perfect black cycle, punctuated with lots of shiny chrome that reflected the sunlight, nearly blinding me. Its swept-back lines lured a kid to go fast. It was inevitable a boy would want to test the posted speed limits.

Mr. Holland was manicuring his lawn. He had been Postmaster for as long as I could remember.

"Mr. Holland, I was wondering if you might want to sell that motorcycle."

"You bet I would. It was a mistake to give this speed demon to Rodney."

"I hear it runs great, but I'm not sure I can afford such a nice motorcycle. What do you want for it?"

"Well, I paid $700 last year. I suppose you heard about all the trouble it caused. You can have it for $150."

"I've been working on a concrete crew making a buck an hour. I have $100 on me right now and could pay the $50 balance over the next few weeks."

"What guarantee do I have that you'll pay me the balance?"

"I give you my word. Here's $100 down payment. I'll pick her up a week from today and make my first payment on the balance."

The next Saturday I caught a ride to town and paid Mr. Holland the first payment, leaving a balance of $30. He trusted me and handed over the signed title. The bike was mine.

Though I'd never driven a motorcycle, I was determined to learn. It took several miles of starts and stops before I figured out where the brake levers, clutch levers, and gearshift levers were located. By the end of the first day, and with only a couple small mishaps, I got the hang of it. It was a bit rough, but I could keep my new ride between my legs.

Noting my past success with the old Ford, I expected to bring home my new toy without any problems on the home front. The fact that my mother had been a "dare-devil" motorcyclist in her younger days didn't raise any red flags for me. How was I to know owning a motorcycle was not an option for her son?

I didn't learn until my arrival that she had been involved in a serious motorcycle accident years before, while riding inside a ball-shaped cage. She had performed this act with another cyclist many times, but her last performance nearly killed her. I vaguely remembered seeing a mangled boot and bloodstained leathers stored in the garage.

Thirty minutes after arriving home with my two-wheeled horse, I was grounded for life, my "steed" parked out back, covered with an Indian blanket. Two weeks later, my life sentence was commuted to time served, but my speed machine remained off limits until the following summer.

Hot, humid, summer days retreated with the fall colors, bringing welcomed cooler breezes. I wasn't allowed to work on Sunday, but was permitted to putt around the country roads in my old Model A. School started on Wednesday and my head filled with thoughts of high school. I was excited about my new adventure, but also scared.

I drove past a "Property For Sale By Owner" sign posted on land near our house. The allure and problems with school dissolved as I fantasized about building a house on this lakeshore lot. I could imagine myself sitting on my porch, as the geese landed on my lake to spend the night before continuing their flight south.

Later that evening, while my parents were outside, I called the phone number listed on the sign. The owner wanted $1,000 for the two lots, and would take $100 down, and $200 per year for four years. He explained that with a Land Contract, I would be the recorded landowner, and he would be the lien holder until the debt was paid in full.

"I'll take it. Can you draw up the paperwork for me and send it to my address?"

"I can do that. I'll send the agreement to you. You will have to sign the document and return it to me in the mail. Don't forget to include the $100."

Mom was curious about the letter that arrived for me a few days later. She wondered about the contents but didn't pry. I had a checking account at a local bank, and decided to seek the advice of Mr. Nelson, the banker.

"Let me get this straight, Dennis. You're a freshman in high school, and you want to buy two lots on a lakeshore. You plan to build a two-bedroom house and want to start construction this fall?"

"Mr. Nelson, I don't play sports because I live too far from town. I work each night after school, and every Saturday. My past purchases include a Ford Model A and a motorcycle. I already have $300 in my checking account here at your bank and don't need a loan. I just want you to look at this agreement and tell me if it looks legal."

"This was prepared by an attorney so it's perfectly legal. It looks like a good deal. I suggest you buy it. Does the seller know that you are only fourteen years old?"

"He didn't ask my age. Does that make a difference?"

"If he hasn't asked, I wouldn't mention it." Mr. Nelson notarized my signature and watched as I wrote the check for $100, the required down payment. "Go mail it, Dennis. You're now a property owner. I've never seen a kid take an interest in buying real estate before. You're a different sort, but I wish you luck. You're going to need it."

A month had passed when Pops and I stopped by a farm auction. The auctioneer was asking for a bid on an old iron-wheeled wheelbarrow. I bid one dollar and someone upped me, then four dollars and was upped again. The auctioneer raised it to six bucks. I nodded. On the way home my Dad asked, "What are your plans for that old wheelbarrow?"

"I'm planning to dig a basement for a new house. I've wanted to tell you this for some time. Last month I bought two building lots down the street. I'm designing a two-bedroom cabin, and want to start digging the basement before the ground freezes."

"Why didn't you tell me about this before now? You know I could have helped you."

"Dad, I will need your help at some time, but I want to do this part by myself. I'd appreciate your help staking out the building. You know, make sure the basement is square. I can't do that alone."

"Not a problem, son. Let's do it next Saturday."

"How about tomorrow?"

"You know we don't work on Sunday. Next Saturday is soon enough. I'll get a bulldozer to move the dirt. That'll save you lots of hard work."

"Are you going to charge me for the dozer?"

"You know better than to ask me that, but I'll make you a good deal."

"I think I'd better dig the basement the hard way. I can afford that."

It took me four years to complete my first house. Upon graduation from high school, I was the proud owner of a two-bedroom house with no debt to my name.

During my high school years, I also worked at the local feedlot three afternoons a week and all day Saturday. The work was hard and paid only sixty-five cents an hour, but I was happy for the job. The owner was a good man, and a good boss. After several months, he came to me with a proposition.

"Dennis, I have lots of heifers in my feed lot. On occasion, they surprise me with a calf. A calf is more unwanted here than a whore in church. I will give you every calf born if you get it off my lot the very day it arrives."

My Dad had built a small barn and some corrals behind our house. Three days later, I was in the "bucket calf" business. I mixed powdered milk and fed those little critters four times a day. Most of the calves were weaklings, but I tried every method I knew to keep them alive. Even with all my good efforts, their fatality rate was still 50%.

Every week I hauled home one or two calves. Each morning I woke up early to care for my herd before school. When the orphans were old enough to wean, I took them to the livestock auction barn. I worked my butt off, and drew pride from the additional $250 my calves brought me each month. I calculated I could make more money working for myself raising the calves than working at the feedlot, but my boss made it clear that the day I quit, the orphan calf supply would also end. I enjoyed the record keeping and data analysis necessary to run my little business. Future Farmers of America honored me with their highest award at the close of my freshman year.

Sometime during that same year, I discovered Flying magazine in my school library. The cover caught my attention, and the articles inside fed my imagination. I determined that day to become a pilot. Dad and I both enjoyed the Sunday afternoons we spent watching airplanes land and takeoff. It shouldn't have been a shock for him when I announced, "I'm going to take flying lessons at the Fremont Airport."

His heated response surprised me. "When you leave home, you can do whatever you want. As long as you live under my roof, you will not get into an airplane. Are you clear about that?"

I determined never to mention flying around the house again, but within a few days, signed up for my first flying lesson. The cost and my demanding workload prevented me from actively pursuing my passion. It took more than a year of lessons before I was ready to solo. My instructor presented me with a permission slip that required a parent's signature before I could fly alone. I took the form home, but kept it in my desk for several weeks. On my 16th birthday, I returned to the airfield with the signed document. The instructor and I made a couple of touch-and-go landings before he told me to taxi back to the office.

"You don't need me anymore, Dennis. Go out there and give me three good landings. Bring it back in one piece."

After some time in the sky alone, I taxied back to the parking area to tie the plane down. *I had done it! My dream was coming true.* The instructor signed my logbook, "OK for solo flights." As I drove toward home, I wished that it was dad that signed the permission form for this special flight, instead of my practiced forgery of his signature.

My flight training progressed on schedule. One Saturday afternoon, while I was flying, my parents shopped near the airport. When they drove past, they recognized my car in the parking lot. Filled with rage, they waited for my return. After finishing my flight, I tied down my plane, and completed the required paperwork, too absorbed with my flying to notice the ambush.

As I opened my car door, a booming voice brought me back to earth. "You are in big trouble, Mister. When you get home, plan on moving out."

I arrived home to silence. My father sat in his favorite chair and didn't look at me. He muttered, "You don't live here anymore. You are on your own now." Usually Dad didn't say much. This time, he said too much.

Later that winter night, I took my rifle and dog, and walked into the woods to my favorite cave. I spent three nights thinking. When I returned, Mom made a compelling case on my behalf for allowing me to return home. Dad was the head of our family, but Mom had a way of getting his attention. Things were never warm between us again. In most respects, I was truly on my own from that time on. Every child comes to a time of decision that propels him toward adulthood. This was my time.

After an afternoon of hunting one fall, and with darkness settling around me, I drove back to town on a country road seldom used. I passed Banker Nelson's Cadillac parked in the weeds along the edge of the road. I stopped and backed up to see if there was some kind of trouble. He rolled down his window.

"Good evening, Mr. Nelson. Are you having car trouble?"

"No, no, it just died. I'm sure it will start in a bit. I was looking at some farm ground when it started acting up."

I walked over to the stranded car feeling confident that I could help. As I reached out to open the door, I noticed Barbara, the mother of a classmate, on her knees, looking for something on the floor.

"Hi, Dennis. I'm looking for my purse. I must have kicked it under my seat. Oh here it is."

"Mr. Nelson, I'll wait until you get it started. I don't want to leave you folks all alone out here." He turned the key. The Cadillac started, and idled perfectly. He got out of his car, tucking in his shirt as he walked me back to my car.

"I appreciate your offer of help, Dennis. You're a fine kid. Can I trust you to keep this car problem a secret?"

"Absolutely, Mr. Nelson. It wouldn't be good for people to know that a brand new Cadillac had engine problems, but I'm sure your mechanic can fix it. Good luck!"

Banker Nelson had always treated me with respect, but I didn't realize how much he cared for me until I filled out my first loan application. It was time to purchase my first airplane and I waited patiently while he looked over the application. He seemed a little nervous. Finally, he pushed back his large, overstuffed chair, staring at me in silence.

I spoke first. "You probably don't have many loan applications from seniors in high school for the purchase of an aircraft. This is a great deal, only $2000 for it. How much do I need for a down payment?"

"Dennis, I've never forgotten the night you went out of your way to assist me when my car wouldn't start. You kept your promise, didn't you?"

"I would never tell anyone your Cadillac was a lemon, Mr. Nelson."

He nodded and looked relieved. "Wait for a moment. I'll be right back." He stepped out of his office for a few minutes and soon returned with a check and piece of paper. "Sign right here, Dennis. You have your airplane."

I was surprised when I looked at the check. "Mr. Nelson, this check is for the full amount of the purchase." I read over the bank note. "No payments due for a full year. How can I thank you for being so kind?"

"You're a sharp kid, Dennis. I'm sure you'll think of something. Enjoy your flying!"

Not yet nineteen, I realized my dreams were within my grasp. I completed high school, unnoticed by most. By overcoming hardships and pursuing my goals, I had acquired a car, a motorcycle, land and a house, and now, an airplane. Opportunities and adventure awaited me. My future looked promising.

I know the plans I have for you; Plans to prosper you and not to harm you; Plans to give you hope and a future.
Jeremiah 29:11

Alaska or Bust

What does it mean to be obsessed?

For me, obsession means being consumed by the vastness of the North, where the sun defies rising in the east and setting in the west. I've been touched forever by huge valleys filled with loneliness, and moved by rivers that flow unrestricted, some milky, others muddy, but most of them clear. I've seen mountains that rise straight up like the fangs of a wolf, touch the sky, pierce the clouds, and then fall to the earth again. Blue and white seas, replete with marine life, have inspired me. I've trespassed on glistening glaciers that melt into rivers and streams filled with ice flows in spring, producing rapids that churn and roar.

I've trodden the delicate purple tundra that keeps its promise to greet the snow each winter when silence sprawls and the northern lights glow. The North is a disease; if you go there, you might catch it. If you catch it, you will never recover. I have the disease. The North calls, and beckons me home.

I married my high school sweetheart, the prettiest girl in school, when I was nineteen. We honeymooned on an island amid a vast frozen lake in Canada. We experienced the splendid emptiness of the North and, together, fell off the known world. The harsh, untamed land enchanted us. We taught Cree Indian children at a school accessible only by airplane and dog team. My airplane was the only one within a 100 mile radius of this remote community.

During our stay in Canada, I flew many lifesaving rescues, and Carol often attended to medical emergencies. Our cabin in the woods nestled along the shore of an island on Lake Winnipeg, one of Canada's largest lakes. It had been home to a lighthouse keeper for many years before we purchased the old cabin, with the land it sat on. A wood-burning cook stove worked hard to prepare meals of moose meat and potatoes, while heating our small home. It also warmed the soles of our feet, as we rested on log chairs after dinner. Carol often read aloud the works of Robert Service, late into the night. As the fire died, the water in the washbasin froze, but we kept warm the way newlyweds do, snuggled under soft down quilts.

Our family and friends thought us mad for what they considered a dreary quest. At their parties and social functions, they expressed concern about our lack of modern conveniences. They never understood that we had lost nothing, but had, in fact, discovered the secret heart of the wild. What they considered loss was our gain. The stillness of the North soothed our souls.

After three years in the Canadian North, my father died unexpectedly, forcing our return to the world of concrete and superficial comforts. We soon realized that electricity and telephones did not rest well with our spirits. It took a couple of years to settle the affairs of my family, but the infection of the North could not be cured by a high-rise society.

"Carol, I'm sick of these groomed malls, and miss my shack in the snow. I long for the Northland and the adventures of the bush. I'd like to move to Alaska. I now understand why birds migrate north each year. They must go. I, too, must return, or I'll shrivel and die here."

"I miss it, too, Honey. Let's plan to go back with the birds in the spring."

"I can't wait. The North is calling. I have to go now."

"Now? It's November. Nobody drives the Alcan Highway in November except escapees from the psych ward."

"I know you're right, Lovie, but I can't wait longer. Let's leave the day after Thanksgiving. We'll drive the Willy and pull the trailer loaded with all our belongings."

"It sounds exciting, and a little scary. You always promised to show me the Great Unknown. I guess I'd better start packing."

We spent the next couple of weeks preparing our Jeep and packing our trailer for the 3,000-mile trek north. I knew no one who had driven the Alcan Highway, so I used my previous experience with the North's cold and prepared for breakdowns, and forced overnights in the bush.

"I swear, Carol. You must have a degree from the Sardine-Packing Institute. You couldn't get one more whisper into this trailer."

"I packed it good and tight, Honey. I put the emergency gear near the rear, so we can get to it easily. All the household goods are stored forward. We won't need them until we arrive in Anchorage. I placed the heavy items, like your tools, over the axle to help balance the trailer. We've got a heavy load, and don't want too much weight on the trailer hitch."

"Good work. Lovie. I'll lash the spare tires for the Jeep and trailer on top. I installed a holder for two gas cans on the back. We'll have ten gallons of emergency fuel, just in case we run short."

I backed the Willy into the trailer and lowered the tongue onto the hitch ball.

"This isn't good. The Jeep springs are nearly mashed flat."

"What does that mean, Dennis?"

"Jeeps aren't built for pulling heavy loads. We have only three inches of clearance between the rear axle and the frame. We still have to load the inside. We'll have to take it slow and easy. We don't want to break an axle on the road."

We packed the last of our belongings on Thanksgiving Day. Between turkey and pumpkin pie, Carol stuffed in the last few items.

"Carol, where are the boys going to ride?"

"Cory can sit between the sleeping bags and the canvas sidewall in the back. Leslie is small enough to sit on my lap, or between the two front seats."

"How can I shift gears with Leslie between the seats?"

"He's only two. How much room will he take? He sleeps a lot of the time. He can lie next to Cory, on top of the sleeping bags. Don't even suggest tying him on top!"

"Oh, give me a break, Carol. I should tie *you* on top. That would provide a lot more space inside."

We left the next morning at the crack of noon. Too many goodbyes and some last minute changes delayed our departure.

"I hate goodbye tears and sniveling, Lovie. We aren't moving to the end of the world."

"Well, Anchorage may not be the end of the world, but I'm sure it can be seen from there. When we arrive in Anchorage, everyone will stop worrying."

"Lovie, it's only 3,000, maybe 3,500 miles away. Let's get on the road."

My wife studied me for a moment, then asked, "Honey, do you really know how far it is to Alaska?"

"Not exactly. I couldn't find a map showing the entire trip. This one takes us to the Canadian border. We'll have to buy a map for Canada when we get there."

Dust from the gravel road leading to the highway waved a final goodbye. We were on our way. After several hours, I realized that Willy was working hard to give me 55 mph.

"I'm glad you didn't pack anything more, Lovie. With this load, this old girl can only produce 45 to 50 mph. We'll take it slow and pray for a safe trip."

At the end of the first day, we had traveled just over 200 miles. I pulled off the highway, and backed our trailer alongside an ancient cottonwood tree growing along the Platte River. The engine wasn't even cooled by the time Carol set up the tent and fluffed the sleeping bags. We were ready to rest. After a quick trip behind the cottonwood tree, we nestled into our warm bags and tried to sleep.

"I can't sleep, Lovie. I wish the sun would hurry and rise. I want to get going."

"Take it easy, wild man! We have a long way to go. It's fall here and the weather is good now, but you and I both know that when we arrive in Canada, winter will be there to greet us."

Youth blinds a person and encourages stupidity. I had hoped to drive twelve to fourteen hours a day, making it possible to arrive in Alaska in about a week. On the third day, in the middle of Montana, winter leaped across the Canadian border and descended upon us.

"I'm glad we have four-wheel drive. I couldn't drive into this campsite without it. I haven't taken my hands off the steering wheel all day, and I'm beat. Lovie, can you set up camp without me?"

"Not a chance. In this wet slushy snow, you'll have to dig down to solid ground before I put the tent up, or we'll be soaked before morning." Carol was "bush savvy," and absolutely right. It took us more than an hour to set up the tent. It stopped snowing by the time we tucked both boys into a down-filled mummy bag. Sleeping together, they kept each other warm. Star confetti appeared as the overcast thinned.

"It's going to get really cold tonight, Dennis. I'm stuffing one sleeping bag inside the other. Cuddling won't cut it tonight."

"You're right, Lovie. I didn't expect this kind of cold until we reached central Alberta. I'll have to heat the Jeep engine in the morning or it won't start."

When sleeping in a down bag in subzero temperatures, it's necessary to remove all your clothes and place them at the bottom near your feet. Sleeping with your clothes on dampens your garments. In the morning, you will freeze in your clothes before you can get warm. Crawling into my cold sleeping bag next to my nearly naked wife was the only joy I experienced that night. Everything else was miserable. Fatigue can be a blessing on a night like this. It dulls discomfort.

I opened one eye and immediately shut it tight. *It must be a cold dream.* Frost coated the inside walls of our canvas tent. Reluctantly, I paused and then opened both eyes to confirm reality. Moisture from our breath decorated every inch of the interior with tiny white frost doilies.

"It's cold in here, Lovie. Stay in bed until I get the Jeep started. Wish I'd brought a thermometer along, but it doesn't matter. It's below zero." I pulled my clothes from the bottom of the bag and labored to put them on.

"Dang! These puppies are cold."

Fully dressed and still in the sleeping bag, I let my body warm some. After a bit, I slipped from the comfort of down and pulled the flap of the bag over Carol's head.

"Lovie, stay warm as long as you can. You don't need to crawl out until you hear the Jeep start."

"Mommy, we're cold. Can we get in your bag?" The boys didn't even wait for an answer. They quickly scooted into Carol's bag and snuggled together like three bears in a down-lined cave.

At the rear of the trailer, I had stored the engine heating equipment: a propane tank, a weed burner, and a four-foot piece of six-inch stovepipe. I slid one end of the stovepipe under the engine oil pan, and then repositioned the lit weed burner in and out of the stovepipe until I found the spot where the air drafted correctly. Warming a frigid engine is not a process that can be hurried. After about an hour, I turned the ignition key. Willy protested but started. I was eager to get back on the road.

"Honey, Willy's running. Let's give it time to warm up and then we'll break camp."

"Come on, boys, let's get dressed. It's frosty in here. Hurry, guys, before we all freeze."

We putted along until we reached the Canadian border near Sweetgrass, Montana. The station guard waited inside to avoid the severe cold. I pulled up to the shack door and started to open the door.

"Stay inside your vehicle," the guard yelled. "I bet you're on your way to Alaska, right?"

"Yes, sir."

"Are all of you American citizens?"

"Three of us are Americans. My oldest son was born in La Paz, Manitoba. He can choose Canadian citizenship someday if he wishes."

"That makes him the lucky one, doesn't it? Are you carrying any contraband? You know, drugs, booze, or a hand gun?"

"No, sir. Nothing like that."

"Okay, you're free to go. Don't freeze up in that thing. You look real cold." The door slammed shut and the officer disappeared from view.

"Dennis, you lied to that guard. We have a handgun in the trailer."

"If I had mentioned that, he would have made us unload everything from that ice box. Does that prospect interest you, Lovie?"

She considered the option for a moment, "I suppose you're right, Honey. Let's get going."

We camped in the snow three more evenings, each night colder than the last. As the temperatures steadily lowered, the process of getting started in the morning took longer, and longer.

"Dennis, I've lost track of the days, but we've been on the road for a long time. Maybe you haven't noticed, but we're starting to smell like a bunch of goats that have been sitting around a campfire. When we get to Prince George, we need to spend a night in a motel."

I sniffed a couple of times. "I don't smell anything, Lovie."

Carol shook her head. "Trust me, you stink!"

"Okay, one night in a motel. We can't afford any more than one."

We arrived in Prince George early that evening. On the northwest side of town, I found a cheap hotel attached to a gas station and a small café.

"Honey, eight dollars for this room seems like a lot of money, so let's make the best of it." Carol managed our money carefully. "Everyone gets a hot bath. Tomorrow, I'll repack everything. I'll dig out all the snowsuits, and we'll wear them inside the Jeep."

"Good idea, Lovie. My knees were freezing all day. How about giving the boys the first bath. Then we can take a bath together after they've gone to bed."

"I can think of several reasons why that might work out just fine."

Maybe that long soak in the tub was too enjoyable because we forgot to set the alarm. It was about 10:00 a.m. when we gathered in the café for our first restaurant meal since leaving Nebraska more than a week earlier. I lit the propane heater to warm the Jeep before heading toward the cafe and hoped the engine would be warm by the time we were ready to leave.

The old man who ran the gas station came into the cafe. When he saw me, he came over to our table. "I'm Drake. Harriett and I own this place. Do you know the weight of the transmission oil you have in your tranny and rear end?"

"I don't have a clue. Why?"

"Harriett said she heard your transmission making a strange noise last night when you pulled in."

"I heard it, too, but I thought it was normal in this cold."

"Maybe not. I have a Jeep the same year as yours. If you're running factory lubrication in the tranny and rear end, it's probably too thick for this weather."

"I've been having trouble shifting between first and second gear."

"I think it might be good to check the fluids before you go any further north."

After breakfast, I backed the trailer into a parking spot and unhooked it. Then Drake and I drove Willy around the parking lot and down the road.

"Hear that high pitched squeal? You've got metal rubbing against metal. You need to change out your lubrications. You may already have some damage."

"Can you take care of this for me in your shop?" I asked Drake.

"Yep, drive it in. I'll put it on the hoist and check it out."

Carol didn't seem disappointed to hear that we might have to spend another night in our knotty pine box. She moved the cold weather gear into the motel room in preparation for the journey later.

Drake unscrewed the drain plug on the transmission. The oil reluctantly found the hole, formed a small black rope, and then crawled into the collection pan.

"Look here, Dennis. The oil is so thick that I can cut it with a knife as it drains. It will take an hour or more to drain the transmission and the rear end."

Actually, it took all afternoon. After the molasses-like contents were collected, Drake heated it on a wood stove. When warmed, it looked like oil again. Drake poured it across newspapers on the floor.

"Look at all the glitter in this, Dennis. Some of these pieces are large enough to read the serial numbers."

"Really?"

"No…but almost. You're lucky you stopped here. You wouldn't have made it to Whitehorse. We'll have to work on it tomorrow. It's quittin time. I'm going home."

The boys, Carol, and I walked to the grocery store about a mile back toward town. "We could be here for a few days, Lovie. Buy only what you must. We better not eat at the cafe anymore. We need to save every penny. I have no idea how much this repair will cost, but I'm afraid we won't have enough money to pay the bill and still make it to Anchorage."

"God knows our needs, Dennis. What will be will be."

Drake's shop looked like a junkyard moved indoors. Drake and I worked on my Jeep for the next two days. Willy had a factory-installed overdrive, an addition to the transmission, allowing higher speeds. One of the gears was damaged because the oil became too thick to circulate to the overdrive box.

"Tell you what I'll do, Dennis. I'll remove the overdrive unit and bolt a plate from my Jeep over the hole in your tranny. I'd like to keep your overdrive unit. If you agree to this exchange, I won't charge you for the repair."

"What would it cost just to repair the damage?"

"Probably between $350 to $400. If you're not interested in a swap, that's fine too."

Without the overdrive, our Jeep would go slower and the trip would take longer, but we would have sufficient money to complete the trip.

"I like the idea of a swap, Drake. You've got a deal."

"Well, that's good. Unbolt the unit and I'll get the cover plate. I'll have you back on the road by morning. Harriett and I would like for you and your family to have dinner with us tonight at the cafe."

"That's real nice of you, Drake. We appreciate your kindness."

At first light the next morning, we turned onto the Alcan and resumed our arduous journey.

"Lovie, this slower pace will make the trip a day or two longer. But it's better to go slow and arrive safe than to hurry and not arrive at all."

"I don't mind going slow, but the cold is starting to wear on me. I'm chilled deep down and can't get warm. This little heater can't compete with this frigid land."

Carol was tough; she seldom complained. Since Prince George, we hadn't seen one day above minus 20. As I drove, Carol kept busy scraping the ice off my window, maintaining a small hole of visibility.

We finally arrived at Watson Lake, and took some time to enjoy Signpost Forest, a park filled with signposts. We left Willy running while the four of us explored. The arrow on each post stated the mileage to a distant city.

"Look at this, Lovie. Here's one pointing to Omaha, Nebraska. Over there is one pointing to Anchorage. We've come a lot farther than we have left to go."

"I'm glad we're on the downhill side of this trip, Dennis. This cold is relentless."

We had traveled a short distance west of Watson Lake when a blizzard snuck in behind us. At first, the flakes came down light and fluffy - nice to see. But soon the wind began to blow, and the visibility diminished to a few hundred feet.

"Lovie, I can't see a thing. But, the semis aren't slowing down at all."

As the big eighteen-wheelers passed, snow whirled around us, blinding me. We were between nowhere and White Horse when one of these monsters forced us off the road. Willy plowed over the snow berm at the edge of the road and came to an abrupt stop in a ditch surrounded by snow six feet deep. The four wheels continued to turn, but Willy wouldn't budge.

"Dennis, I think we're in big trouble. You came close to upsetting Willy. What are we going to do now?"

"I'm not sure, Lovie. I guess I'll just have to dig us out. There's no one out here to help us."

The heavy snow made it difficult to open the canvas door. When I finally managed to push it wide enough to squeeze through, I stepped into waist-deep snow.

It looked impossible to dig Willy out. Through the blinding snow appeared the lights of a northbound eighteen-wheeler. The roar of his engine died as the airbrakes engaged. The big truck stopped on the road ahead of our Jeep, and the driver jumped from the cab. He jerked open the big doors of his trailer and pulled out a long steel cable.

"Hey, Kid. Fasten this cable to your frame. Get in your vehicle and leave it in neutral."

I complied and jumped back in behind the wheel. The cable tightened, and without a jerk, Willy moved forward until we sat back on the Alcan.

"There you go. Now try to keep it between the ditches."

"Hold on a minute. How can I repay you?"

"You can't. Return the favor someday by helping another traveler in trouble."

He returned to his truck. The big engine growled, and within a hundred feet, his trailer lights disappeared into the blizzard.

"Dennis, do you believe what just happened?"

"Not yet, maybe some kind of miracle. I would have paid him for helping, but he wouldn't hear of it. We'll make it to White Horse tonight. Let's find a motel room and get warm."

"Honey, I think that trucker was an angel, incognito."

The storm had abated by the time we arrived in Whitehorse. Though the snow continued to fall, the wind had blown itself out. Most motels were closed during the winter months, but I finally found an old log complex on a side street. Next to the motel sat a decaying log cabin. A brass plaque nailed to the front of the structure read, "Home of Sam McGee." On this frigid eve, I understood why Sam had wanted to be cremated.

We were chilled to the bone and couldn't go on without some rest. The room was shabby and worn, but after a hot bath, it felt like a palace.

"Lovie, I'm going to let the Jeep run all night. I won't have to take extra time to heat it in the morning. Tomorrow, we can get an early start."

"Good idea, if you think it's safe to do that."

I rose early the next morning after a night of blessed sleep. The rest had renewed my strength. I cracked open the door to check on Willy and heard the sewing machine engine tapping out a tune. *Good little Jeep!*

As I opened the door to our shabby accommodation, an ice cloud rushed into the room forming a ghostly shape that hung around the entry until the warmth of the room made it disappear.

"It's awfully cold out there, Carol. This is the coldest so far. You and the boys stay warm in here while I load the Jeep and check everything for our departure. We can be out of here in a few minutes."

I placed all of our stuff inside Willy, and then popped the hood to check the engine. I was shocked to see a large wasp nest attached to the underside, something

I'd never witnessed before. In the dim light, I was uncertain what it was and hesitated to touch it. When I poked it with my pocketknife, the blade penetrated the pile with little resistance. It was coagulated oil droplets. The temperature had dropped so low that the oil had been pushed out of the air breather hole one drop at a time, and adhered to the underside of the hood, forming a dark brown football-sized blob.

"Lovie, get me a pan." I cut the strange oil formation away from the hood and watched as it fell into the pan.

"What is that, Dennis?"

"It's frozen oil. Take it inside and put the pan in hot water."

Carol wrinkled her nose in disgust. "It looks like calves' liver."

"Maybe, but I wouldn't eat it."

In about twenty minutes, the coagulated mass became liquid again. I poured it back in the oil fill-hole and added a quart of new oil for good luck.

"Lovie, I'm not going to stop until we make it to Anchorage. We've seen cold before in Manitoba, but I've never seen it this severe."

"Anchorage is more than 700 miles away, Dennis. That's sixteen to twenty hours of driving. Can you stay awake that long?"

"Your job is to keep me going. I'm sure you'll think of something to help me stay alert."

In a few minutes we were back on the Alcan, rolling west. Sometime during the night, the falling snow surrendered to clear skies. Carol continually scraped to keep a hole open so I could see to drive. We were freezing inside, but hadn't considered how this cold affected the metal parts outside until the left trailer spring broke with a sharp crack! The fender dropped against the tire and we could go no farther.

"Dennis, can you fix this?"

"I saw a milepost marker on the hilltop behind us. I'm going to use the wood saw to cut it off at snow level. I think it will fit between the axle and the trailer frame to hold the fender up above the tire. We won't have a spring on the left side of the trailer, so we'll have to drive even slower. Hopefully, my idea will work."

Milepost markers were originally set every mile from Dawson Creek to Fairbanks. The 6-inch x 6-inch posts with chamfered tops were four feet above the ground. Each was painted white and had a black milepost number. Milepost 1106 fell to my saw. I hoisted my trophy on my shoulder and walked back to the Jeep.

Smoke rose near the edge of the road as Carol bent over a small fire cooking something. Within a dozen paces, I caught a waft of something scrumptious baking over smudgy willow embers.

"Lovie, is that bannock I smell?"

"The boys were hungry so I stirred some up. Would you like a wedge?"

"You don't have to ask me that question. I want a big piece. Do we have any canned milk?"

"There are several cans between the front seats, but they're probably frozen."

I cut the top off a can of Pet Evaporated Milk and scooped out the frozen contents.

"Hey, boys, come get some of this. It tastes like cake and ice cream."

Bannock is a staple of the Canadian north. It's a flat biscuit-like bread, usually baked outside in an open skillet facing a hot fire. Carol could build a fire, stir up the bannock, and take it steaming hot from the skillet in less than twenty minutes. This was the first batch she had prepared on this trip; it was a special treat. The temperature remained extremely cold, but somehow I felt warmer with fresh bannock going down.

I used a wood chisel to notch the post and position it snugly where the bolt protruded from the axle. Using our heavy-duty jack, I raised the trailer frame and fitted the 6 x 6 post over the bolts, then lowered the frame until it sat solidly on the timber. Four screwdrivers driven into the post on both sides of the spring secured the milepost marker in place.

"Lovie, I think it'll hold. Kick snow on the coals and let's give it a try."

I checked the fix several times. My innovative repair held fast.

The dim light of morning returned as we drove into Muldoon, only a few miles from Anchorage. We had been on the road for 24 hours, without stopping to rest. Upon arriving in Anchorage, we noticed the marquee at the First National Bank blinking the time and temperature.

"Lovie, look at that! It's minus 44, and it feels warm. Thank God, we made it!"

By afternoon, we found a two-bedroom apartment in Eagle River, about 15 miles east of Anchorage. We threw our few belongings on the floor, turned up the heat, and soaked in a hot tub until our skin felt real again. It was December 18th. We had spent 21 days on the road, most in the cursed cold. Alaska was now our home.

We approached Christmas broke and far from family and friends, but we were blessed with youth and each other. Carol covered some cardboard boxes with red Christmas paper, transforming them into festive end tables. I found some rough-sawed lumber at a swap meet and fashioned a small picnic table with benches. We were happy in our new home.

Before Christmas, we drove Willy north to hunt caribou and spruce hens. On our way home, we cut down a spindly spruce tree for our living room and decorated it with homemade ornaments. Carol prepared caribou roast for our Christmas dinner.

Our gifts for the boys were simple and inexpensive, but they loved each one. On Christmas morning, a present wrapped with a big bow waited outside in the cold. They heard the yipping, opened the gift, and hugged the Malamute puppy with happy hearts. Carol and I exchanged hugs and hand-written love notes. They meant more than any store-bought gifts.

Carol had saved enough money to buy the ingredients for homemade eggnog, starting a family tradition that yet continues. None of us missed the decorated malls. We were blessed with a warm, loving holiday season that is etched forever in our memories.

I held my wife close to my heart. "If being broke brings us this kind of Christmas, I choose to remain broke forever. Merry Christmas, Lovie. Alaska's our home now."

The week between Christmas and New Year's Day, I visited every business that operated airplanes for hire. On the third of January, I received an offer from Deadhorse to fly a Cessna 185 on wheel skis. At this time, Deadhorse was the main base for all North Slope drilling activities.

"Lovie, I'll be gone for four weeks, home one week, and then gone for another four."

"Is there any chance we can move up there with you?"

"No, Lovie, they don't allow ladies or children to live on oil field sites."

Wien Airline's Boeing 737 landed on the frozen gravel runway and taxied to a complex of modular buildings. The plane that I would pilot sat in a snow bank along one side of the facility. I learned later that it hadn't flown for several weeks. The previous pilot had been killed in a flying accident, and I was his replacement, an important detail my new employer neglected to tell me.

This time of year, the sun never clears the horizon. Without its presence, the rays flowing over the Brooks Range to the south provide only twilight at midday. By the time I received a room assignment and transported my gear, it was too dark to ready my plane for flight.

I wanted to call my boss to learn more of the previous pilot's demise. I also needed to express my concern over the poor condition of my aircraft. The communication system on the North Slope was HF radio, erratic at best. When the northern lights glowed, radios wouldn't transmit at all. Although the radio was manned twenty-four hours a day, messages were relayed for only an hour or two each day, and transmitted according to priority established by the oil company. I knew my message would lie near the bottom of the list.

I spent the next day digging snow from my aircraft. Upon opening the pilot door, I was disappointed to find the white stuff had drifted into the cockpit through a gap in the rubber window seal. The rock-hard snow packed up to the seat cushions. In a couple of more weeks, the snow would have completely filled the plane.

The engine had a cover, designed to maintain warmth, but it did little to keep out the snow. I opened the cowling and found snow crammed in around the engine. It took the entire day to dig out the plane and remove the ice. After warming the cockpit and engine compartment with several electric heaters, I tied the engine cover around the cowling to slow the heat from escaping. I removed the aircraft battery and took it to my room to thaw out. The next morning was the beginning of an adventure that lasted for many years.

***

"It's good to be home, Lovie. I have amazing stories to tell. I've landed in areas uninhabited and untouched by man. I've never seen so much wild game."

On our way home, Carol told me about her exciting discovery. "Do you know that we can acquire land like the old homesteaders? We find a parcel of land to build a cabin on, stake our claim, and file it with the Department of Natural Resources. In a couple of years, the land is ours."

"How did you hear about this?" I asked.

"When I was in Anchorage, I stopped by the McKay Building. The DNR office is in the basement. There was a posted notice telling about land available and the process for filing."

"I'll check it out tomorrow. Tonight we're going out for dinner and a movie. What movie would the boys like to see?"

That week home from the slope, Carol and I read everything available about Open to Entry Land, referred to as OTE. I'd heard of a village where three rivers meet. Talkeetna is on a dead-end road, fifteen miles off the Parks Highway, about 120 miles from Anchorage. The Susitna, Chulitna, and Talkeetna Rivers come together in a large basin near there. The Alaskan Railroad passes through, providing accessible transportation to the outlying areas.

"Lovie, this area looks interesting. When I come back next month, let's spend a couple of nights in Talkeetna."

"Sounds great to me, Dennis. I'll be ready to leave the day you get back from the slope."

My next time off came during the first week of March. Carol met me at Anchorage International Airport. As we walked back to the Jeep, she shared the information she had found.

"I asked around about Talkeetna," she told me. "They say that there's not much there. We may not be able to find a place to stay. There's a motel called the Tee Pee, and an old Roadhouse. The gal at DNR said they may not be open during the winter months."

I shrugged my shoulders. "I'm sure we'll find something. I want to check it out."

Carol smiled. She knew me. "Well then, we're packed and ready to go."

After bear hugs from the boys, the four of us set out on another adventure. Snow berms six-feet high lined both sides of the narrow two-lane highway. After traveling several hours, we arrived in Talkeetna. A hand-painted sign near an old log cabin read, "Welcome to Beautiful Downtown Talkeetna." The population was 85. Scowling gray skies hung to the treetops. A 12-foot pile of snow leaned up against a yellow house across from the Fairview Inn, an old historic bar. Another weathered frame building with an uneven roofline rose above the dirty snow.

"Look, Lovie. There's the Talkeetna Roadhouse."

Carol squinted to read the sign. "I think it's closed, Dennis. I don't see anyone around."

"I'll check to see if the door is open." I was determined to look inside.

When I turned the knob and pushed the door, it swung open. Behind the counter, next to a large wood cook stove was an old man of slight build. His white hair accented his ashen skin.

"Can I help you?" he asked in a deliberate tone.

"I'd like a room for two nights. I'm here with my wife and two sons."

The old man studied me for a moment and then asked, "Are they well behaved? I don't have rooms for little terrors."

"They're perfect little guys. They won't cause any problems, I promise. My wife can be a problem at times, but I can control her." I smiled at the old man, but he didn't smile back.

"I hope you're joking. Find a room down that hall. They're all vacant. If you want to eat supper, come back at 5:30. We serve right at 5:30 sharp. If you're late, you don't eat."

At the appointed time, we walked to the dining area, and sat down at the large table. There were mounds of food, served family-style. Ham and potatoes, prepared on the old cook stove, were heaped on large platters. Thick slices of fresh, homemade bread sat near a tempting selection of small glass bowls filled with jams.

"I'm Dennis and this is my wife, Carol. My older son is Cory. The little guy's Leslie."

"Well, I'm Carroll with two rs and two ls," the old man said. "My wife Verna is in the kitchen. Eat up now. You can have all you want, but make sure you eat everything you take."

Dinner was delightful. When we finished our fine meal, the table was cleared and we chatted with our hosts. They poured dark coffee and served white cake for dessert. Carroll and Verna Close were a bit coarse and direct in their conversation, but we sensed hearts of gold. Before bedtime, our boys had taken to the old couple as if they were their grandparents.

"I lock the door at 10:00 p.m. sharp. Make sure you're inside before it closes. I won't come back downstairs after I go to bed."

At 10:00 p.m. Carroll wedged a large butcher knife into the trim around the door near the knob.

"Is that the lock for your door, Carroll?"

"Yep. It's done the job for years. Make sure you turn the lights off in the sitting room before you retire."

He and Verna retreated to their room upstairs.

Carol turned to me and whispered, "Honey, I love this place. I could live here indefinitely." She had found a home away from home.

The smell of breakfast cooking aroused us the next morning. Sunlight filtered through the window. We had slept in.

"Lovie, I'll eat whatever they're preparing downstairs. The aroma is intoxicating and I'm hungry." I started to get out of bed but Carol tugged at my arm.

"The boys are still asleep. Let's pull the blanket over our heads and stay in bed a bit longer."

Such an invitation was hard to pass up, but the aroma of fresh coffee wafted past our room. I pushed back the heavy blankets.

"I can't wait, Lovie. I'm going down for a fresh cup of coffee."

"Okay, I'll go with you."

We sat on bar stools behind the counter near the old cook stove. Carroll poured two cups of heart starter and we chatted together. Verna sliced one-inch thick slabs of homemade bread. She flicked water onto the top of the stove; the drops sizzled and evaporated. Then she lightly sprinkled salt over the hot surface and plopped the thick slices on top to toast.

"Breakfast is in ten minutes. Better get up your boys if they want to eat."

The boys always loved breakfast, but this day they looked sleepy as they stumbled into the dining room. When Leslie spied Carroll, he trotted over and threw his little arms around the old man's waist.

"Leslie, thank you for that hug. It's been a long time since I'd had such a big one from a little guy. When your mom and dad go back to Anchorage, why don't you stay here with Verna and me? We could use a little helper."

Carroll picked up Les and put him in a chair next to the big table. Verna brought breakfast in large platters and bowls: scrambled eggs, ham, Texas toast with lots of jam, and Donald Duck orange juice. As we enjoyed our bush breakfast, Carroll and Verna related stories about the area and their experiences running the Roadhouse for the past thirty years.

After breakfast, Carol wanted to help with the dishes. Verna declined.

"I appreciate your offer to help, but we have our own way of gettin things done around here. The dishes are my job, but you could pick up in the sitting room and shake out the rugs. I'm getting too old to move the furniture."

Carol brightened at the chance to help out. "I'd be glad to do that for you, Verna. I enjoy house cleaning."

"Well, in that case, we'll give that room a good spring cleaning together. I've been meaning to do that for some time."

Carol and Verna were determined to kill the dirt and make things shine. I took the boys outside for a walk. I figured the women would stay busy for a couple hours.

I discovered that Talkeetna has two landing strips located a short distance from each other. The long runway lies east of town, across the railroad tracks, and was cleared of snow down to the gravel. FAA employees lived in a dozen government-style houses that sat on a street perpendicular to the runway. They maintained the landing strip and manned the airport radio. Twenty-five percent of Talkeetna's population lived in these FAA homes. Used primarily for fueling aircraft in route to destinations farther north, this airport lacked local aircraft.

As we walked past the B & K Trading Post, a yellow and red Super Cub floated a few feet above the Fairview Inn on approach for landing on the Village Strip. The skis slapped down on the frozen runway. The pilot made a turn and taxied back to the road where we stood. I hadn't noticed this little strip the day before, the most fascinating I'd seen. Super Cubs tucked between the trees on both sides of the narrow runway, which ran from the center of town to the bank of the frozen Susitna River. The boys and I walked the entire length and counted six planes snuggled in the brush among the trees.

I was excited about what I had found. "Carol, I want you to see the runway just down the street. The planes land right in the middle of town."

Old Carroll piped up, "You should check out the old log building on that runway. Years ago it was a livery stable. A lady bought it and fixed it up. It's not in the greatest condition, but I think she wants to rent or sell it."

My wife and I walked back to the town strip and found the old building, vacant, with snow piled up to the eaves. With a little work, it could be livable.

"Lovie, I'll be going back to the slope in a couple of days. While I'm gone, check about renting this old house."

"This community has its charm, Dennis, but I'm not sure we want to live here. We're settled in Eagle River. Let's give it some time before we make another move."

I wanted to please my wife, but this opportunity was hard to resist.

"Carol, I want to start my own flying business someday. This would be a good place to begin. There's not much happening here now, but this place is bound to grow."

We had to head home the next day. Reluctantly, we packed up and exchanged goodbyes with Carroll and Verna. The morning was bright and clear, with a blue sky and small cotton ball clouds drifting overhead.

"Carol, let's walk down to the Talkeetna River before we leave. Verna says it's only a block north. If we're lucky, we might be able to see Mt. McKinley."

Upon arriving at the river's edge, the base of the huge mountain stood clearly visible, while the peak hid among the clouds.

"Dennis, I wish we could see the top of Mt. McKinley."

Then the clouds began to lift. We watched quietly as the mountain slowly came into view. The rock and ice monolith filled the horizon, as the clouds encircled the summit like a crown.

"Dennis, I've never dreamed of anything so spectacular. We are truly standing at the foot of the throne of God."

White snow with vertical black lines defined the mountain's rock fields and glacier moraines in contrast to the brilliant blue sky. God had blessed us with a special viewing. Before we left, the clouds descended again like a curtain. The majesty of the mountain was gone - at least for today.

We were nearly back to Eagle River when Carol said, "Honey, I'll talk to the lady who owns the old log house on the Village Strip. Maybe we can rent it. There's something special about Talkeetna."

I smiled at her, realizing she felt the magic of that place too.

I remained on the North Slope until the end of May. With each day the ice and snow melted, making it difficult to find a place to land. The Cessna 185 was overdue for maintenance. It was time to load the equipment and my gear on board and head for Anchorage. Flying along the proposed pipeline route, I stopped in Fairbanks for fuel. From there, I followed the Parks Highway to Healy and Cantwell, planning to land in Talkeetna for more fuel. This was my first flight over the Talkeetna area; it was gorgeous country. The Susitna River spreads a mile wide where the Chulitna and Talkeetna Rivers converge. The green foliage reflected life, after seven months of dormancy. I filled up my plane at the long runway and spent some time talking with the fueler.

"I heard that the old log house on the Village Strip was rented to a lady with two little boys. Don't know why they'd be moving here."

"What do you know about this lady, Shorty?"

"They say she's young, has two little guys and drives a Jeep. Says her husband is a pilot on the North Slope for some oil company."

Carol didn't know when to expect me home. She had planned to surprise me with our new home in Talkeetna. *That little stinker! I'll fix her.* I lifted off the runway and made a pass over the Village Strip. Our Jeep sat in the driveway next to the log house. The boys played in the backyard with their half-grown puppy. *I wonder how Carol thought she could keep this a secret.*

I flew on to Anchorage International and delivered the Cessna to the maintenance shop. Across the street was Reeve's Credit Union. I opened an account and deposited six paychecks. I had found a deal on a Super Cub the last time in town, so I took a cab to the hangar at Lake Hood where the plane was tied down. The "For Sale" sign still peered from the window. This was the plane I wanted. I stepped inside the small office and wrote a check for the purchase price. Thirty minutes later, I taxied to the gravel runway near Lake Hood.

The Talkeetna Village Strip was wet, and mud splashed onto the bottom of the wings as I touched down. After a U-turn on the runway, I taxied into the driveway swinging a wingtip over the Jeep hood. Carol appeared startled to see a Super Cub in her driveway, but she nearly fainted when I climbed out.

"Honey, what are you doing here? And where did you get that little plane?"

"I discovered your little secret, Lovie. I just bought this plane in Anchorage an hour ago. The North Slope is closing down for the summer. You and I just went into the flying business."

Carol had moved our few possessions into the log house. In a couple of weeks, she had transformed the house into a comfy and inviting home. The boys were glad to have their daddy back and greeted me with hugs and more hugs. We were a family again and had a real home!

We enjoyed a meal that night with Carroll and Verna Close at the Roadhouse.

"I want to thank both of you for telling us about the old log house and encouraging us to move to Talkeetna."

"On a good day, we can see the biggest mountain this side of heaven," Carol added.

This might be heaven, I thought, as I gazed at my family. Heaven or not, it was our new home.

Horse and Sleigh

Carol and I had acquired teaching positions on the Cree Indian Reservation at Cross Lake, Manitoba. It was the second Friday of January 1967, my students finally settled down, and started their first assignment of the day. I slipped out of the classroom into the furnace room and filled the firebox with as many logs as it would hold. Then I worked my way back to my desk and started on my lesson plans for the next week.

Moments later I saw two Cree ladies hurrying toward the school's entrance door. Desperation gripped their faces. I recognized the old Cree woman and a much younger Metis girl, probably in her late teens. I knew the way of the people: the older woman had something to tell me, but her English was as poor as my Cree, and she had brought the younger girl to help convey the message.

I left the classroom and met them in the entrance where the kids hung their coats. The younger girl was too excited to talk slowly. She could speak English but she was so distraught that every other word came out in Cree. I understood that there had been an accident with an ax, and someone was hurt. A few minutes into this effort, I was relieved to see Charlie Sinclair, the local chief and a good friend, come through the same door. Charlie was always composed, and I could understand his English with no problems. He told me that the daughter of the old Cree woman was splitting firewood when she missed a swing with the ax and hit her foot. She was badly hurt and bleeding profusely.

The nurses' station just down the trail provided emergency care, but the head nurse had not yet returned from her holiday, and the underlings were not capable of handling a wound of this nature. Charlie wanted me to fly the injured lady to the Wabowden Hospital, but the weather was nasty. The temperature hovered at 30 below, with a light snow falling, limiting visibility to about a mile.

Then there was the issue of having to heat the aircraft before it could fly. As I made my case for refusing the mission, other family members pulled the injured lady to the schoolhouse on a toboggan. This was a very serious injury. The ax had been sharp; the glancing blow struck her foot just behind the big toe and opened a gash to the heel. These people had no first aid training, and the wound was not even bound. Blood squirted over the snow, revealing a blood trail all the way from the nurses' station. Charlie translated their frustrated conversation and told me that the nurse's assistant at the station was not capable of treating the lady.

It was time for a decision. If I flew the lady to Wabowden, she would live. If I didn't take the trip, she would probably die. At that moment, I never considered that I might not make it to Wabowden, or that we both might die. I decided to fly.

Carol and I moved to this remote Indian community after being hired by the superintendent of the Frontier School Division. Carol taught grades one through three in the church next to the school; I ran to advise her of the situation. We moved the kids from the church and put them in the school building. Carol had some first aid training, and wrapped the wound tightly with strips of sheets. She must have put 10 layers of wrapping around the foot attempting to stop the bleeding. I eyed the injured foot as Carol prepared the young woman for flight. The dressing was already blood soaked.

Charlie helped me get the Citabria heated and ready for the flight. At 30 below, this was not a quick process. After each landing, I raised the toe of the ski and slid a log under it to prevent the ski from freezing to the snow. This also made it easier to slide a stovepipe and elbow in the hole under the back of the engine cowling. Charlie and I installed the stovepipe and started the propane weed burner, a skill I learned years earlier. I pushed the weed burner in or out of the stove pipe opening and find a point where it drew just right, pumping heat to the back of the engine.

At this temperature, the moment the warm air hits the cold aircraft parts, they turn white with thick frost. This is also true for the metal inside the engine. The piston walls gained about a half inch of frost on all sides, and the aircraft can't start until the inside walls are dry. When the frost melted and the metal appeared dry, I covered the engine cowling with old blankets to hold in the heat, and then turned down the weed burner so the engine didn't get too hot and melt some wires or plastic parts. I left one bug eye hole in the engine cowling open so the moisture could escape. This process can't be hurried, and considering the injury, I kept my eye on the deteriorating weather and decreasing visibility.

It seemed like hours, but in reality it probably took about one. This wasn't the time to start the engine before it was ready; I needed it to start. If it didn't start on the first try, the frost inside the pistons would turn to water. If the water hadn't completely evaporated during the heating process, the moisture would foul the spark plugs and they would have to be removed and cleaned before the next attempt. I had learned that the inside of the engine was dry when I couldn't find any wet areas on the outside of the engine. I gave it about ten more minutes.

When it was ready, Charlie and I removed the logs from under the skis, threw aside the old blankets and I reached through the door and primed the engine. I turned the mag switch to *both*, ran the throttle forward and back several times, reached from behind the propeller and swung it down. It popped and exploded to a roar. We would fly!

Carol and Charlie helped load the old Cree woman and the patient. As I climbed into my pilot's seat, someone handed in a baby wrapped in a blanket. The baby was laid in the luggage area behind the back seat. " I'm not bringing that baby on this trip," I protested.

I was informed that the injured lady was the baby's mother; there was no one to nurse the baby while she was gone to Wabowden. It was hopeless to argue.

Moments later, I started my take-off on the very spot where the Citabria had been parked. I had less than a mile of visibility and only three years of experience as a bush pilot. As long as nothing changed, and I didn't miss a turn in direction, we would arrive Wabowden in about an hour. In those days, there were no radios, or radio aids of any kind. I learned to navigate by using a continuous stream of landmarks. As long as the landmark stream was unbroken, and I had good visibility to the ground, I could make it to my destination.

The Citabria became airborne after a few hundred feet, and I climbed to about 200 feet altitude. I flew down the Nelson River to the first fork, and then took a slight left turn to parallel the predominant tree line on top a ridge. This heading led me to the burned forest area, where I made another slight left turn that pointed me to the south end of an unnamed lake. From that landmark, I navigated by using a drainage, with heavy trees along its banks. I leveled the wings and waited. In a few minutes I crossed the railroad tracks that led to Churchill, then a gravel road, and an immediate 45-degree left turn.

If correct in my bush navigation, I was now on final approach to land at the local airdrome. Flying downwind was never good for landing, but with a 20-knot wind and low visibility, it was safer to land downwind than to maneuver for a landing into the wind. Visibility was now less than one-half mile, and the end of the runway was coming into view. There was a ski-equipped Beaver aircraft lifting off about mid-runway. *Not good!* I hadn't thought about another fool out flying in this crap.

I banked hard right and he went under me with two layers of paint to spare. I banked hard left and saw him disappear into the snow showers. With the runway ahead of me again, I chopped the power and headed for the landing area. The plane slid along the frozen snow right up to the dock area, just as if I planned it that way. But, in fact, I hadn't even seen the dock area when I first touched down.

Cross Lake didn't have a radio that worked that day, so no one in Wabowden knew about me or the injured lady on board. I bailed out of the plane, ran to the road, and flagged down a car. In a few minutes, several cars and people showed up to help me extract the young lady from the plane. Everyone spoke Cree and hurried about. In less than two minutes, I stood alone next to my airplane, with nary a soul in sight.

The weather was still one-half mile visibility, but I knew the way and was ready to return home. Down the runway, and I was off. I climbed to about 200 feet, made my 45-degree right turn, watched the gravel road go by, and then the railroad tracks. In just a few minutes, I picked up a tree-lined drainage and turned toward the south end of the unnamed lake. But something was wrong! The drainage didn't look right. In addition, I had learned over the years how to read sunlight rays, and the rays' angle to my flight path seemed wrong.

I paralleled the wrong drainage and I knew it, but was I north or south of my desired flight path? The old-style whiskey compass proved worthless in these northern latitudes. I picked a point on my right wing tip, turned to half of that heading, and waited to see if I recognized any landmarks. The rays of sunlight seemed correct, but I could only see straight down. Nothing looked familiar to me, and it was time for the sun to drop below the horizon. I had less than an hour to make it to Cross Lake before dark. If I lost twilight, I would have to find a place to land, regardless of my location.

I had no IFR instruments in this aircraft and needed good visibility to stay on course. I tried not to think about my lack of survival gear, removed earlier to make room for the passengers. I considered turning back to Wabowden. But where was back? If I turned around, the odds of missing the small village behind me seemed greater than missing Cross Lake if I continued. I chose to trust my instincts and pushed on.

Well, Lord, it's just me and You, and this is looking like a serious situation. I'll do what I believe is best, but whatever the result, it's all Yours now. Whatever the outcome, I put my faith in You.

Relying on gut instincts and the angle of the sun's rays, I fixed my heading, leveled my wings and prayed for Cross Lake to appear below me in about 40 minutes. Thinking about the decisions I'd made, I began to regret some of them. I wasn't forced to take this trip. The woman might have survived her injury. So, what made me feel responsible for this woman's life? Was I a hero, or a crass fool? Who pulled the sleeping bags out of the plane? How could I've been so stupid to take a flight without survival gear? It seemed like the right thing to do, but now I questioned every aspect of the flight. A guy can beat himself up at a time like this, and that may be good. When a pilot makes a poor decision and survives, the experience causes him to make better choices the next time.

It was getting dark. I hadn't seen a recognizable landmark for the entire flight, and the end of the day was near. Visibility was less than half a mile. Flying just above the trees, I spotted some frozen water—a river or lake below. I was shocked to see a black horse pulling a sleigh loaded with firewood. It passed underneath me in a direction about 50 degrees to my right. A horse and a sleigh going in that direction meant that someone must live there. I banked to the sleigh's heading and followed the ice path for several minutes, then throttled back, slowed down, and prepared to land. Wherever I was, I had to land. Only minutes remained before total darkness would make landing impossible. Suddenly, I saw a light! It was dim, but it was there. Then another light and another.

Good Lord, I'm over the Nelson River and there's Cross Lake. I chopped the throttle, smacked the frozen river with the skis, and taxied about a mile to the very spot I had left earlier that day. Flinging open the door, I wanted to jump out in victory. Then I realized it wasn't my victory. My knees shook; my limbs were too weak to move. I slumped over the stick and trembled. I would have missed Cross Lake if I had not seen the horse and sleigh.

Thank you, Lord. I wouldn't have made it here without You. I sat in the plane for some time trying to regain composure. No one came to meet me. When I was able to walk, I made my way to the house and stumbled inside.

Carol looked relieved, "Honey, I'm so glad that you're home." She reached out and gave me a warm hug. I leaned against her for support; I still felt shaky.

"You should be glad, I made it. I wouldn't have if it hadn't been for that horse and sleigh about five miles west of us. If I hadn't seen them, I'd be lost out there in the bush."

"I knew you'd make it home," Carol assured me. "I was praying for you."

The next morning at about 10:00, Charlie Sinclair knocked on my door. He came in and sat in his usual place, the big over-stuffed chair in the living room.

"I so glad you take injured lady to Wabowden. She in big trouble."

"That's okay, Charlie. She'll be better soon. They'll take good care of her at the hospital."

"Weather bad for flying. You have trouble getting back to Cross Lake?"

"I almost didn't make it. I would have missed Cross Lake if that horse and sleigh hadn't appeared just in time."

He leaned forward. "You saw horse and sleigh in the bush? What they look like?"

I described the black horse and faded red sleigh that I had seen heading toward the village. I related how I had turned toward Cross Lake upon seeing them.

Charlie paused for a long time, looking directly into my face. He spoke slowly. "That was old Sam and his horse Blackie. Old Sam and Blackie die years ago. Never been another horse around here since."

I learned weeks later that the injured woman would walk again. She would always limp a little, but still had both feet. Except for Charlie's expression of thanks, no one ever mentioned that rescue again.

Cold

Alaska has four seasons: June, July, August, and winter. The warm months of endless sunshine supply comfort and allow time to prepare for winter's survival. Rivers aflop with fish, and mountainsides gorged with berries provide ample stores for the hardy folk resolved to withstand the ice age attack.

Men of snow, like me, know the cursed cold will come. The glacial weather moves my direction, determined to overtake me. In early September, the first evidence of winter is pleasant. It would be inviting if I didn't know what lurked behind. Leaves of gold and red descend to their fragrant grave, carpeting the forest floor. The scent of high bush cranberries and ripening rose hips perfume the fall air.

Cold reality arrives one morning when I walk to the boat dock and drop my pail into the lake. *Thud*. It lies dead and unfilled atop clear ice. The warmth is gone and won't return for nine months. Winter has begun; each day trudges toward colder weather. We people of the North fight the cold; if we live, we win.

I never squander the warm days. In addition to gathering food, I fell a forest of firewood, and pull the logs to the cabin, where they are left to dry. Later, they are cut to length, then split and stacked in piles higher than my head. The bottom rows are lost in mid winter, when twelve feet of snow blankets the earth. My outdoor efforts to defeat winter continue until the cadaverous cold forces me inside. It's a dreary rest. Now, I'm forced to remain in a log bunker deprived of sunlight and bludgeoned with Arctic blasts.

During the first week of December, people who live in the "Lower 48" are thinking of a white Christmas. They envision winter, remembering experiences from places like Aspen and Vail, where frost spangled air fills the enormous valleys, and the mountainsides are awash in bright sun. Visitors slide down the white fleece with their jackets open and the wind blowing in their hair. Designer sunglasses and Rolex watches accent their attire.

The winter scene I experience is not inviting. I haven't felt a warm sun since late October. It now arrives and departs just above the southern tree line.

Saddened by skies of forlorn gray covering its face, I yearn for the season of long shadows.

Alaskans are thankful for the holiday season, and the joys that brighten our otherwise dark days. The winter solstice, the shortest day of the year, initiates the festivities. With each successive day, the sun will begin hanging around longer. It's a good reason to celebrate.

Many of us meet in Talkeetna and stay with friends for Christmas. Some fly in from their gold mines, others walk in from the remote Upper Talkeetna River, and a few flag down the Alaska Railroad for a ride to town.

Every night bush people in soiled blue jeans and "bunny" boots, many with smoky beards, whoop it up at the Fairview Inn, with loud music provided by local artists playing banjos, guitars and flutes.

Talkeetna Christian Center on Main Street focuses on the "reason for the season." The church plans several special events. Nearly everyone in town shows up for the Christmas play, where they watch children transformed into angels, shepherds and sometimes a sheep or donkey. Christmas Eve service by candlelight is special. We sing the carols with gusto, and enjoy extraordinary Yuletide music performed by talented musicians who often write a special piece to celebrate. The ladies of the church spend hours baking and decorating festive cookies and cakes that are served with coffee and homemade eggnog. The church opens its doors to house the bush people who camp on the floor in down sleeping bags.

On Christmas Day, many return to the church at noon to eat Christmas dinner, shared with anyone who wants to come. The feast is prepared by the church people, and by anyone who wishes to contribute. It's a sight to behold. Moose roasts, turkey, ham, and baked goose with all the trimmings entice all to overeat. People of the bush, out of necessity, eat simple meals, so this celebration is enjoyed to the fullest. We all understand that such excess and generosity will not be shared for another year.

The New Year's Eve talent show starts at 6:00 p.m. The performances are unusual and often funny, composed of plays, bands, readings, jigs, and old time "jam sessions." Participants and the audience love the entertainment and continue the show past the midnight hour, laughing and eating until we're exhausted.

With the New Year's celebration over, Carol and the boys depart to visit family in the "lower 48," while I'm left in our little cabin to face old man winter alone. The party is over and reality returns, bringing the onset of regret. I can't understand why it continues to get colder each day, even though the daylight hours increase. *Goodbye, sweet joy. Good morning, dreaded cold. You've come to stay a while longer.*

It's the latter part of January—not yet 2:30 in the afternoon—and the sun has already peaked, and now fades into the southern horizon. Distant trees form a thin black line dividing the sky from the snow. Earlier in the day, the sun had been obscured by a haze of suspended ice crystals, but now they've moved away, allowing the last rays of daylight to reach over the horizon, revealing a bleak and bitter land. From my window I gaze at hues of gray and black. Any breeze has stilled. It's so quiet I can hear the temperature drop. *It's here. When the light disappears, the attack will begin. Cold, cursed cold. I wish I could beat it back, but I can't.*

In the North, temperature isn't a number painted on a stick next to a glass tube. Up here, the old-timers often refer to a thermometer as a whiskey stick, or a mercury stick. Cheechakos measure cold in numbers. Sourdoughs measure it with what they see and feel. I am now a seasoned veteran of the Arctic; I know this will be a night to remember.

From time to time, I hear a person refer to a "three dog" night, a night when it's so cold you have to sleep with three dogs in order to stay warm. I tried it once and it *ain't* as good as it sounds. I couldn't keep the dogs in bed, and, at one point, the huskies went at each other, nearly ripping off my face. A week later, I discovered a colony of fleas in my long johns. Tonight would be a "three dog" night, but I plan to stay warm without the dogs.

I stock the wood box and pile more firewood on the floor next to it. When no more will fit inside, I swing the door closed. A quick check of the mercury stick through the window shows 32. *That's minus 32.* At this time of the year, nobody bothers to say "minus," since it's never above zero. Cheechakos would say it is 32 degrees below zero Fahrenheit.

The cabin's occasional creaks and groans tell me the night's cold has begun its attack. An indigo sky decorated with bright stars provides a faint light, reflected off a blanket of snow. Like me, the moon hides from the cold.

It's best not to go outside on such a frigid night. Looking out my window in the faded light, I'm startled by a sudden flash in the sky. As bright as lightning, the Northern Lights sweep in bars across the lake and illuminate the distant shoreline. Shimmering ribbons of blue, green, and red form a gigantic curtain, pulled across the lake by the hand of God. After a few spectacular minutes, the lights vanish; the show is over.

Frost forms around the edge of the windowpane. Tiny frost doilies knit by Mother Nature, or perhaps Jack Frost spread slowly across the surface. The individual patterns join as they grow in size. Like snowflakes, no two are alike. The delicate-looking patterns on the pane defy removal. Any attempt to scrape a hole in the white barrier is futile. It quickly knits again, as though no intrusion was made.

I estimate the temperature has dropped to 40 below, and have a method to prove it. I remove the steaming teapot from the wood burner and fill a 12-

once glass to the rim with boiling water. Swinging wide the door, I pitch the hot water into the inky sky. Instantly, a hissing sound explodes, similar to pouring water on a hot woodstove. A cloud appears over my head and then I hear the soft tinkling of bells. It's the music played by ice particles colliding in space. The icy mist hangs motionless above the roofline for a moment, but soon joins the smoke from the chimney to form a tail that trails toward the lake. Not a single drop of water falls to the snow. I've performed this trick dozens of times. At 38 below, the experiment is a wet failure. A quick check of the stick; it's 40 below. I've always wondered if there was a scientific reason for this phenomenon. Perhaps the meeting point of -40 Fahrenheit and -40 Celsius on the thermometer is significant.

Back inside the cabin it's impossible to ignore the cold radiating from the walls. The doily-covered windows are no longer lacey white. The frost has been transformed into ice nearly an inch thick. The smoke from the Coleman light attaches to the icy buildup, casting a dirty yellow hue. Where there was a harmless window hours earlier, a block of ice now trespasses into my living area.

Frost grows in the top four corners of the cabin. Frosty stars cover the ceiling. The cold has found the metal nails that hold the shingles to the roof and follows them inside seeking the heat. Without exception, every nail grows a white tuft of hair. Hundreds of them reflect light from the gas lantern, as if the heavens have moved inside. If it weren't for the bitter cold moving in with them, it would be a lovely sight.

My surroundings freeze around me, but I find the door the most fascinating. The knob on the humble latch is now white and as large as a softball. The door hinges protrude into the cabin like two half-blocks of ice. The cold seeping through the crack eventually builds sufficient ice to make it impossible to open the door. It will be sealed tight until this assault has ended. There's no need to check the stick. It's at least 50 below.

I fill the airtight with all the wood I can jam inside, and then open the damper and flue. The airtight is a sheet metal stove, with metal about the thickness of a pop can. A red spot about the size of a biscuit grows on each side of the tin stove. It looks inviting, but the warmth of the radiating heat reaches only a few feet. Directly above the stove, the temperature is above freezing but everywhere else the air is frigid. I pull my chair as close to the wood burner as I dare, and wrap myself in a couple of caribou robes.

I'd been dozing when I hear the first "rifle;" the sound slaps me awake. "Rifle" is the term used by old timers in this part of the North to describe the loud bang a tree or rock makes when the cold freezes the moisture inside. The frozen object can no longer expand without bursting; the explosion sounds like a shot from a 30.06 rifle. The first crack is somewhere deep in the woods, but soon trees near my cabin join in. It's time to fill the stove again. As I push in the last log, I lose count of the number of "rifles" breaking the silence of the cold night. The forest has come alive. The cabin joins in with a few bursts of its own. I feel the snap against my moose hide soles, but reassure myself that I'm safer inside than outside.

It has to be at least 60 below to hear the forest protesting the bitterness. I heat a butter knife on the stove and scrape a small hole in the windowpane. The mercury, now a frozen ball at the end of the stick, confirms my speculation. *If I spend another winter here, I'm purchasing a more accurate thermometer. I bet it's near 70.* The icy hole in the pane disappears. There's no need to look again.

At times like this, there's only one thing left to do. I'll have another cup of coffee and hunker down. I find my cup on the floor, but my java is a solid mass with a frozen crown adorning it. There will be no more warmth tonight.

Deep in my down sleeping bag, with the caribou robes pulled over my head; my last slumbering thoughts warm me. *Thank you Lord, spring is only ninety days away*.

Dog Boy

It was late November, and despite what the calendar indicated, winter was here. The snow piled two feet deep, and the moving red dot on the thermometer hadn't nudged above freezing for more than six weeks. Winter is expected in Alaska, hell it is Alaska, but I didn't expect to see *him*.

He came out of the B&K Trading Post, slipping from shadow to shadow. It was his garb that caught my attention: many layers of clothing, all mud-crusted rags. Three or four scarves circled his neck. His hat was an old bomber's cap, with the earflaps pulled down and tied under his chin. Large holes in the knees of his trousers revealed the layers beneath. The only skin exposed was his face and hands, and they were filthy, and disgusting: crusted with dirt, campfire smoke and soot. Yet, I could see he was very young.

I walk into the B&K to ask about this strange boy.

"Kris who was that, or what was that?"

"I don't know, DB. He's been in a couple of times the last few weeks. He's a real sad sight. Did you smell him? I almost gag whenever he comes in, and each time it gets worse. He buys very little, and he always pays in coins, no bills. Look at these. They're the old kind. You know, the ones without a copper center."

The strange kid had spent less than five dollars, paying with half dollars, quarters, dimes and pennies.

"What did he buy, Kris?"

"He bought Krusteaz pancake mix, a box of wooden matches, and a pound of butter. Nothing else."

"We have some eighty people in town and you and I know every one of them. Who could he belong to?"

"I don't know, DB. I don't think he belongs here at all. I can't get him to say ten words. Either he's simple or crazy. I'm betting crazy."

"Guess we'll have to wait and see. Give me a gallon of milk, Kris, and a gallon of Butter Brickel ice cream. Put it on my bill. If you find out anything more about that kid, let me know. It's getting too cold outside to survive. He'll have to move on or freeze. Hope we don't find him next spring in a snow drift."

During the time Kris and I chatted, daylight faded. Although I lived only a block from the B&K, by the time

I walked home it was "bitch black"—about 3:30pm. The Northern Lights danced a little to the northwest of the house. Not an impressive display, just a little winter teaser as the sun sank south and reflected its light over the horizon, lighting ice crystals suspended in the northwest sky. Still, it was nice to see.

Carol was in the kitchen, her arms white to the elbows, kneading rolls for dinner, while moose meat and a small salmon loaf baked in the oven. She pushed the salmon on us because we had plenty, and more. We grew tired of salmon faster than moose meat, and Carol encouraged us to eat some with our moose steak, potatoes, and fresh bread with rose hip butter - the typical Alaskan winter dinner menu.

After our meal, I threw another log in the wood burner, and filled my bowl with a couple of scoops of the Butter Brickle ice cream. Two St. Paulie Girl beers topped off "dessert" as Carol and I settled into our evening chairs. TV would come to Talkeetna in about ten more years, but tonight we watched the snowfall, ate ice cream, and drank beer.

I told Carol about the strange person I had seen leaving the B&K. Although Kris had mentioned him a few weeks earlier, Carol didn't think it was unusual that he purchased supplies with silver coins. Copper-centered coins had only arrived in our area a few years earlier, so people still used the old coins up here. To me, however, it seemed strange that the kid spent only coins.

"Kris is worried about this kid because he looks so young," Carol's face revealed concern. "She says he doesn't look any older than twelve or thirteen, and wonders who's caring for him. I'll bet he's living in the woods with some old 'bush rat.' I'm going to meet this kid. He needs a mother's touch."

I knew what this meant. Carol wanted to bring home another stray. In our many years in Alaska, we always had one or more stray people or animals hanging around.

"By the way, Honey, did you hear that another sled dog disappeared? It was one of Coyote's dogs this time. He says that it got loose during the night and didn't come back." Since freeze-up, three or four dogs had gone missing from their stakes. None had returned.

"That doesn't sound like that big a deal to me, Carol. Coyote's got at least twenty dogs staked out, and he takes poor care of them. I'm surprised they don't all run off."

"They say the dog didn't break its chain or pull up the stake. The snap was released, the same as the other missing dogs."

A week had passed when Carol met me at the airport, after I taxied in from a charter flight. " I saw him. I saw the dog boy. I tried to talk to him but he wouldn't say a word. He looked at me in a strange way. I think maybe he's deaf, but Kris says he can talk when he wants to."

"Where did you see him?"

"Inside the B&K, and Kris is right! He stinks like fire smoke and filth. It's really disgusting."

"So, why do you call him Dog Boy?"

"Well, he smells like a dog, and he had a sled dog with him, a real mangy beast, little more than skin and bones. You know, come to think of it, that dog was covered with dried mud also. Where would you find mud this time of the year?"

"I don't know, Lovie. The snow is more than four feet deep, and I've not seen the red dot above zero for the last week. You couldn't dig to mud if you wanted to."

Talkeetna was on the trapping route for many old sourdoughs. Each winter most of them would stop in at the B&K for supplies, or to sell their pelts. While in town, they depended upon Kris to catch up on all the details of the latest happenings. The B&K was the only post for more than 75 miles in any direction, and good gossip was better than a sale any day.

When I stopped by the store later to pick up a few things for Carol, Kris motioned me over. "DB, Trapper Kermit came in here hoppin' mad. You know, all the old trappers hide their cabins in the bush as best they can. He wouldn't tell me where his cabin is, just somewhere along the Talkeetna River, but he said someone got in. He figures it was some Cheechako. He's missing his old .22 rifle and four boxes of ammunition. They stole his pancake mix, all his flour, and three tins of orange marmalade. I told him to file a police report, but he refused."

The State Trooper comes into town about six times a year. Besides, the Trooper would ask where his cabin was located and Kermit would never tell. Old trappers trusted no one.

"Kris, I'll bet someone exploring along the Talkeetna River stumbled across Trapper Kermit's cabin and took whatever they could carry."

"I don't think so, DB. I think it was Dog Boy."

"Dog Boy! What makes you say that?"

"He was in here the other day and bought some .22 shells and a box of Krusteaz. He's never purchased bullets before. And there's something else. More dogs are missing, some mutts that people threw scraps to, but they're gone. And DB, each time I see Dog Boy, he has a different dog tied on a string to that post outside."

"What do you think Dog Boy is doing with all these mutts? Trying to sell them to mushers?"

"Nope, I think he's eatin' those dogs."

"Kris, that's the single, dumbest thing you've ever come up with."

"I don't think so. Now that the weather is getting colder, he comes in here every other day, but the only thing he buys is pancake mix. Do you think he's feeding those dogs pancakes? I doubt it. He's always covered with mud and dried blood. My guess is that he's butchering them. I'll tell you something else. It's not likely he can bring down a moose with those .22 shells."

A day or two later, I went over to Colonel Johnson's cabin to light his stove because he was too old to light it himself. He had been gone from the village for several months, and just returned—boiling mad. Seems some "no good" broke into the cabin while he was away.

"That varmint ate up all my stores and then put his dirty dishes in the sink. He even slept in my bed, and left it filthy. I've been collecting silver coins for years. Were hidden in an old box under a loose board in the floor. He took them all! Maybe you could check around town and see if anyone has seen some of my coins."

I lit the Colonel's stove and stayed until the cabin warmed. Then I trudged back to the house through the snow, now five feet deep. The Northern Lights danced gracefully. I glanced at the red dot as I went into the house—minus 32! Spring was still four months away.

Carol and I talked about the Colonel and his missing coins. We concluded that Dog Boy had been a mystery long enough. Carol's response didn't surprise me.

"I'll keep my eyes open for Dog Boy. He sounds desperate. When I find him, he's coming home with me."

The next morning, a neighbor, who stopped by for morning coffee, found the old man lying dead in his bed. Johnson was a real colonel, but no one knew how long he'd lived in Talkeetna. According to the old timers, he had always been here. Now he was dead.

I helped dig his grave the following day, a real feat, digging in six feet of frozen ground. About a dozen of us said our last goodbyes. Then just like that, the Colonel was gone forever.

After a charter flight, I walked back home. The sun hung below the horizon at 4:30 in the afternoon, but there was still good light in the sky. *Thank God, the days are getting longer.*

I started into the house, but Carol flung open the door and pushed me back. "I've got him, you can't come in right now. He's real upset." At the bottom of the steps lay a pile of filthy rags crusted with mud and blood. Carol had Dog Boy.

I walked back to the airport and called her from the office phone.

"Honey, give me some time to deal with him," she pleaded. "I've got my hands full right now. I'll call you when it's time for you to come home." After about four hours she gave me the OK, so I walked back to the house. The filthy pile of clothes at the back door was gone.

"Tell me what happened."

"I had just stepped into the B&K when Kris motioned me toward the back room. As I walked past her, she mouthed, 'He's here.' I took a few more steps and then smelled him. He looked at me and then down at the floor. He tried to get around me, but I blocked his escape. I had his attention. 'You're coming home with me.' He shook his head 'no,' but I reached out and grabbed his arm. 'You're coming home with me right now.' He looked at me and said nothing. He followed me home without a word."

Carol prepared him some tea, and warm toast with jam. He'd wolfed down three servings before he talked.

"Honey, his name is Dave. He said he ran away from home. He won't tell me where home is. It took me two hours to convince him to take a bath. He was afraid of losing his clothes, so I told him I would wash them and have them ready when he finished with his bath. He was in the tub for nearly an hour. There's no way I could get the smell out of those clothes, so I tossed them in the wood burner while he was in the tub. When he finished, I gave him a pair of pajamas and some house slippers. I promised him some clean clothes in the morning. He's sleeping out in the shed tonight."

"He'll probably run off before morning."

"I doubt it. He hasn't got any clothes and it's minus 25."

Carol was right, as usual. The next morning Dave sat at the breakfast table, with Carol and me, and our two sons, Cory and Leslie. He didn't say much at first, but that morning he became our third son. Carol bought him new clothes, and in a few days enrolled him in school. He lived with us until he graduated from high school.

Nine months passed before Carol learned more of Dave's story. He was number eight, the last child of a struggling family. When Dave was twelve years old, his mother died on Thanksgiving Day. A short time later, he ran away from home and headed for Alaska. He lived on his own for eight months, holed up in a cave along the Talkeetna River. Dave would stay in vacant cabins when he found one, and kept as many dogs as he could find, or steal. He slept with the dogs to keep warm, and when the need arose, they became a source of food. As it turned out, at the time Carol brought him home, he was out of dogs and ideas.

Dave became an accomplished trapper; and ate fried coyote or fox when necessary. Carol wouldn't prepare that meal, so he'd prepare it himself. Dave returned the .22 rifle to Trapper Kermit's cabin in the spring. As to Colonel Johnson's coins, I thought it best to forget the matter. He was gone and had no kin.

Dave worked in our flying business after we took him in, fueling airplanes and helicopters. Whenever there was a vacant seat, he made sure he was on board. When Dave was sixteen, he received his student pilot's license, and at eighteen earned his private pilot's certificate. We allowed him to fly our boys and other kids to Anchorage for a movie, or just for fun - a 115-mile trip each way, in a $200,000 aircraft. After Dave graduated from high school, he attended flying school in the states, where he received all his pilot licenses, including a helicopter rating. Upon his return to Talkeetna, he was the youngest bush pilot in Alaska!

When I grew older and left the state, Dave stayed on and became a famous bush pilot, and the owner of Talkeetna Air Taxi. "Dog Boy" logged thousands of landings on Mt. McKinley, married the prettiest girl in town, and now has three children.

Carol saved his life and I gave him a career. He still considers Carol his mom.

"Bearly" Coffee

Coffee is the lubrication that keeps old bush pilots moving during winter months. Today's flight required I be well oiled. A helicopter charter flight was scheduled to transport two biologists up to the head of the Susitna River to look for a collared brown bear sow. It was mid February; the snow was deep, and the bear would be "denned up."

This wasn't my first bear hunt so after my third cup, I filled my two big Stanley thermoses with strong black coffee, and threw four biscuits in my flight bag together with my favorite large handled coffee mug. I favored this java holder because I could hold it with heavy mittens, and the thick wall kept the coffee warm longer. When we arrived at the den, I expected to sit for hours while the biologists did their work, so I wanted to be comfortable. Thoroughly lubricated, and with my flight bag in hand, I arrived at the helicopter - my office with a large window on the top floor. I personally picked the view each day.

With the helicopter pulled out of the heated hangar, I filled her with fuel, crawled into the left seat, and spun her up. The turbine engine whined, and the blades flapped as the heater pumped massive amounts of hot air into the frigid cockpit. When she was good and warm, I shut her down and poured myself another cup of bush pilot brew.

I was still working on the last half inch of coffee when the back door of my Jet Ranger opened. The two biologists approached from the back of the hangar so I didn't see them arrive. We stuffed several bags of biological instruments into the cargo hold, where I also stored the survival equipment. The men strapped snow shovels to the cargo rack and threw their rifles on the back seat. They secured a small scale in the right front seat and then fastened their seatbelts. Each biologist held a thermos, probably "biologist lubrication." We each poured a cup before I air taxied to the runway, and with a little forward cyclic, my airspeed climbed and we were underway.

Off the north end of the runway, I caught the Talkeetna River and followed it to Clear Creek, then up Clear Creek until it ran into the flatlands above tree line, where at this time of year, not even a caribou can be found.

Turning to a 45 degree heading, I waited to see the Susitna River come into view. I looked for the long shadows cast by the sun just above the southern horizon, shadows that resulted from rock formations or snowdrifts, blocking the sun's rays. In this vast white country the shadows help me navigate.

The previous spring, summer, and fall, I flew these same biologists on darting expeditions. The process works like this: When a bear is located, it usually runs, so I slow the helicopter and pull in a little collective. The airspeed goes to almost zero while we climb to about 200 feet above the ground. This permits the biologists adequate time to ready a special tranquilizing rifle and gives the bear time to decide which direction to run. Big animals don't try to hide from a helicopter.

Usually, a bear runs into the wind or uphill; allowing it to escape temporarily, which reduces the fright and lessens the stress. Using this method, few animals escape. With the bear out in front of me, and when the shooter is ready, I slowly fly up to the bear. The shooter fires the rifle, and sticks the dart in the bear's rump. I became so skilled at this, we could have completed the procedure without the rifle. The previous flying season, 167 bears had been darted; not a single animal escaped.

The tranquilizer is released into the bear, and works quickly to immobilize the animal. The animal is not asleep, just unable to move. As soon as it looks safe, I land next to the bear and a biologist measures the animal, draws blood samples, puts a tag in its ear, and sometimes takes a small tooth. On some, we install a collar with a built-in radio transmitter around its neck. The transmitter emits a signal for about a year. With this special radio, I can home in on the frequency and find the animal in a short time. Each bear is given a frequency kept by the biologist. Occasionally, an animal removes the radio collar and I find only the transmitter. Sometimes, I locate the signal on a dead animal, but most of the time collars are attached to a healthy animal. The animal always remembers me.

Keep in mind, the bear, though tranquilized, is not asleep. It can smell me, feel me as I touch it, and see me as I work over it. Once animals have been darted, they are much harder to dart again. I don't anticipate any problem. Though I darted this brown bear sow last summer, today, she will be asleep in her den.

About thirty minutes into the one-hour flight, I tightened the friction knob on the collective (the control in my left hand), and poured myself another cup of black coffee.

"This coffee is really good!"

Before completing my drink, the radio alerts me to the bear's frequency, or at least her collar. A shallow turn to the left and I lock in on her. Soon I fly over her den and the needle swings, pointing behind me. I mentally mark the location where the needle reversed direction, and fly over the bear again. When the needle reverses once more, I mark the spot.

After four or five passes, the three of us locate the den. On the south side of the Susitna River, facing north, she had picked a spot where the snow would drift deep. Old sow bears like these dens because they are warmer, allowing the bears to wake later in the spring. What usually arouses a hibernating bear is water seeping into the den from the spring melt. This old sow had picked well, and if she had cubs, they were well protected.

I land the helicopter in front of the den. The snow is soft, so to prevent the helicopter from settling up to its belly, and possibly striking the tail rotor, I make several landings on the intended spot to compact the snow. When it was packed sufficiently to hold my weight, I shut her down.

Since there are only two snow shovels, and I wouldn't butt in on another person's work, I pour myself another cup of brew, eat a biscuit, and, from my all-glass office window, watch the biologists dig out the sow's den. It was minus 20. Those guys didn't need me. In truth, at minus 20, they were more comfortable working than I was sitting in my cold helicopter. In a short time I begin to stiffen up, so with mittens on, I pour myself another cup and nibble on another biscuit.

The biologists knew exactly what they were doing - this wasn't their first bear hunt either. They found the exact spot of the den with their hand-held radio receiver, and, within an hour, they dug a snow tunnel into the bear's den.

One of the biologists crawled out and shouted, "She's in there and I'm sure she has offspring." They gave each other a high five, and me a thumb's up, walked back to the helicopter and crawled into the back seat. I lit the turbine engine and pumped heat into the cockpit as they discussed plans.

It takes more than just a little courage to crawl into a bear's den, steal her cub or cubs, examine them, and record their data. They would also examine the mama brown bear, and record as much data as a person could from a sleeping giant. After returning the cubs to the den, the two men would retreat undiscovered. At least, that was the plan.

We each raised our cups and sipped more coffee to bolster their courage. Minutes later, the helicopter blades coasted to a stop and the biologists made their way toward the den. One man carried a gunnysack for the cubs - if there were any - while the other toted a rifle. Courage is one thing, but they always prepared for the worst.

The biologist with the gunnysack got down on his knees and paused for a moment. He looked like he was praying. Then he disappeared into the tunnel. I quit breathing! *Oh, my gosh! How long before that guy comes out of that bruin's cave?*

It seemed like hours, but soon he returned to daylight with a wiggling gunnysack. He placed the sack on the snow, opened it up, and there they were: two brown bear cubs about the size of eight-week old Labrador puppies. The cubs squirmed, wiggled, and tried to crawl away. Although they never stopped squalling, the pair didn't appear the least bit vicious.

Watching this bear wrestling match from the safety of my chopper provided me with considerable amusement. But then, one of the biologists picked up a cub, held it with both hands, walked to the door of my helicopter, and pulled it open.

He shoved the cub inside the door. "Here, DB, hang onto this wiggler while I get some data from his sibling."

"Holy smoke, will he bite?"

"Probably not. Just hold him."

I set my coffee cup between my legs and gripped the cub around his chest with both hands. The door slammed shut. The little guy was a squirming ball of chocolate brown fur. I had to hold on tight or I would lose him in the cockpit. He looked directly at me, his nose only eight inches from mine, not the least bit scared. I, however, was terrified. The cub had dark black eyes, a moist black nose, and a white star patch of hair on his chest. His little pink tongue filled his mouth and was visible each time he bawled for help. He was a cute little guy. By the time the biologist came to retrieve him, I wished I could take him home for my two boys.

Once again, I filled my half-full coffee cup, regained my composure, and hoped the cub wasn't as traumatized as I was. When they completed their work with the cubs, both biologists crawled into the den, each carrying a cub, with some of their gear tied to a rope. From the safety of my cockpit, I watched the procession disappear.

In a short time, the men reappeared in the now dwindling daylight, and collapsed the tunnel so the cubs couldn't escape without their mom. One of the biologists raised his hand above his head and made a circle motion, so I got the heat pumping once again. After they loaded their equipment and strapped themselves onto the back seat, I pulled pitch and headed home.

The sun disappeared below the horizon, but there was plenty of twilight for a safe return to Talkeetna. Somewhere during our return flight, we toasted our coffee cups to a successful mission. *I must have had too much coffee today. It's beginning to taste like shit!*

The rotating beacon appeared at the Talkeetna airport, and then the runway lights. I ran though my "Before Landing Check List," placing all the switches and levers in their correct positions, then gulped down my last half cup of lubrication so I could stow my coffee mug before landing. And there it was in the bottom of my coffee cup.

"Bear poop!" I said with total disgust.

"What'd you say, DB?" Ron, the lead scientist, yelled at me over the rotor noise.

"Uh…uh, air scoop," I said, making up a flying term. "No problem. I'll adjust for it."

He nodded, "Yea, whatever."

Not wanting to become fodder for the latest joke around Talkeetna, I didn't fess up about the event for years.

Later that night, Carol offered me a cup of her latest flavored coffee.

"No thank you, Lovie. I've had all the flavored coffee I can stand for a long time!" and waved the steaming mug away.

"Really?" She looked puzzled and asked, "Was it a real tough day out there?"

I nodded, and said, "Yea, Lovie, a real bear."

Ill Wind

A Chinook is a warm wind that comes to the far north at least once every winter. It usually appears unexpectedly, lasts for one to three days, and upon its departure, returns the North Country to the subzero temperatures that proceeded its arrival. Old timers call a Chinook an "ill wind" because it's not uncommon for a Chinook to raise the temperature 60 degrees or more in a few hours.

The old sourdoughs thought these warm spells brought the flu sickness. A Chinook would weaken the lake ice and often lured "Cheechakos" into the wilderness with the promise of warm weather, only to snap back to subzero without warning, leaving them in desperate straights, or frozen dead in the cold.

It was the last week of February. We had not seen a day above zero for more than two months. When I walked to the office that morning, the thermometer on the post near the hangar door read minus 31. Three hours later, the same gauge read plus 48 and melting snow poured from the hangar eaves. The sky was a deep blue, without a white puff anywhere. A gentle breeze had brought us the warm weather.

This was the most sudden Chinook I had seen in 15 years. I walked back to the house in the late afternoon without my parka. Puddles of water formed on top of the frozen road. All the way home I hoped that somehow this warm weather would last until spring. I was depressed with the long cold spell we experienced for the last two months. *Damn what the old timers say about an ill wind! I love it warm.*

Sometime after dinner, I dug out last year's gardening magazines and started planning my wildflower garden. With all my years' experience in the North, you would think I'd know better than to be so deceived. In truth, I longed for spring. A warm fantasy is better than cold reality any day.

I threw two more logs in the wood stove and turned off the radio. It was about 10:30 and time for bed. I checked the thermometer before retiring and discovered the bad news before I looked out the window. Damn! Frost formed on the corners of the pane. The Chinook was over. I glanced at the temperature reader: plus 17. Reality was back. I wished the Chinook could have stayed a few more days. Oh, well, surely my bed would be warm.

We had one phone in the house, located in the kitchen. At 5:45 a.m., it started ringing. Nobody in their right mind was awake at this hour, this time of year.

"Let it ring, Lovie. If you pull the blanket over your head, you won't be able to hear it. It's probably a wrong number." After 10 or more rings, all was quiet again. But within a minute or so, the phone rang again.

"Stay in bed, Lovie, I'll get it. Don't move. I'll be right back"

It was Dorothy Jones; I wouldn't make it back to bed this morning. The old timers' saying proved true again. The Chinook had convinced a parent of two kids to allow them to cross-country ski from Trapper Creek to Talkeetna, just a couple of miles across the Susitna River. They left Trapper Creek before lunchtime yesterday and should have arrived at Talkeetna in about an hour and a half. The mom never checked on the children until late last night; and they had not arrived.

The State Trooper and Search and Rescue personnel were already at Trapper Creek waiting for the weather to improve. During the night, it had deteriorated; the temperature dropped below zero, and the wind gusted 50 to 60 mph. The cold temperature wasn't unusual, but this wind was the strongest I'd seen in Talkeetna.

At first light, the search teams set out at the spot where the two skiers left Trapper Creek for Talkeetna.

They found nothing, but the tracking dog picked up a scent.

The kids had started from their home in the bush near Trapper Creek and cross-country skied to the river's edge. About half way to Talkeetna a ground blizzard blew in, and they probably lost their direction due to poor visibility. If they had packed a compass, or had been more experienced, perhaps they would have arrived unruffled.

I received a telephone call from Alaska State Trooper, Roger Coffee, saying the tracking dog had lost the trail where the kids returned to the bush on the west bank of the Susitna River. The snow now drifted heavily, and the tracker was unable to find a scent, or a track. Another problem developed: The tracker's radio started to weaken as the cold depleted battery power. The weather had become so nasty ground search parties still waited in Trapper Creek. Now there was a tracker with his dog, plus two kids lost in the worst storm the area had ever seen. The temperature plummeted to minus 20, with occasional gusts to 70 mph. The kids had already spent one night in the bush, wearing lightweight spring coats and carrying no survival gear. No one survived these conditions.

Reluctantly, most of the search team returned to Anchorage. The others accepted the dreaded reality at the local restaurant over a cup of coffee. Just 20 hours earlier, we enjoyed one of the nicest spring days ever witnessed in February, but now the worst storm ever raged, the wind chill 98 degrees below zero. It was sad, but just another cold fact that the Arctic delivers to foolish mortals. Those kids were gone!

A couple of hours had passed since the rescue teams departed. The local ambulance had been stowed back at its barn when Roger received a call on his hand held radio from the tracker, whom most of the crew had forgotten was still out there. His signal was weak, but he reported his dog found a scent - no tracks or other sign, but he was sure the relentless dog was on their trail. This was an experienced, well-trained animal.

Roger told the tracker the rescue team had given up and gone home, and advised the man to return to Trapper Creek. But he refused to quit searching, proving himself to be as relentless as his dog.

Seems the animal had broken its leash, would not return to his handler, and continued to search for the kids. The handler would not return without his dog. The weak radio signal faded; communication was lost. Roger related to me that the tracker was about four miles south of Trapper Creek and still moving south when he lost contact. Roger felt there was only a slim chance the kids were still alive, and knew the tracker was equipped with only enough gear to last one night. If this storm lasted a few more days, we could lose them all.

"Is there any chance you can fly a helicopter out to the location, take a look for the kids, and bring back the tracker before it's too late?"

This was a "Red Rider" call and I hated them. Remember the old Red Rider movies? Red Rider would ride in during a time of disaster, save the day, and then ride back to safety, unscathed. It was a nice movie, but far from reality. No pilot of sane mind would fly an aircraft in gale winds, 200 feet above the ground with less than a mile visibility, searching for lost souls.

"I'm sorry Roger, it's just not possible. If I try this flight, you might very well have four dead people out there."

I was uneasy with the decision, but being dead seemed so permanent. I truly didn't know any pilot with the skills required to fly in this weather. Besides, skill is only half the battle. Aircraft rip apart in weather like this.

I had just hung up when Dave Lee walked into the hangar. "I've never seen this much wind before. I can just barely see the rotating beacon. We must be down to three-quarter mile vis. This is bad!"

"Dave, call over and ask Dick what he's calling the ceiling and visibility."

Dave made a quick call to the tower and inquired. "DB, Dick is calling it 200 overcast and one mile visibility. The wind is down the runway at 60, with gusts to 70, and the temp is minus 27."

"That's gale wind. I've never seen it like this here before. Too bad about those kids getting caught in this crap. I'm glad I'm not out there."

"DB, Dick told me more about the kids out there. Did you know that they're 'Little Bit's' kids?"

"I never thought to ask who they were. Get me the sectional and topo map for the area and we'll try to locate their position. Those kids started out at Trapper Creek. Roger just said the tracker reported a scent four miles south. If it is their scent, and if they kept moving, they would be about seven miles south of Trapper Creek between the river and the highway. Damn it! 'Little Bit's' kids.; I just saw them a month ago."

'Little Bit' was a single mom, and you probably guessed, just a little thing. She worked every job she could find to keep food on the table and clothes on their backs. She was a great mom; this had to be killing her.

"Dave, pull out the Cessna 206 and 86 Yankee. We're going to find those kids. If they're alive, it would be a miracle. Either way, we *will* find them."

"Are you crazy, DB? I can't fly in this."

" I can't either, Dave. Did you plan on living forever?"

"Never thought of it like that."

"To tell you the truth, Dave, I don't think you can fly the Cessna in this much wind without it coming apart. Just pull out the helicopter. I've got to try."

"If you're going, I'm going too, DB."

"OK, pull the helicopter out first and keep it behind the hangar to the east of the door. Pull the Cessna out, engine first. Keep the tail against the door. The lee side of the wind will give us the greatest protection. I'll bring the trucks around. I want you to tie a wing to each truck."

It was a fight to get the Cessna in location and tie it to the pickups, one to each wing. I pulled the fuel hose to the Cessna and filled her with every drop of fuel I could stuff in. Full fuel tanks make an aircraft wing more rigid, and the added weight would help stabilize the plane - in flight or on the ground. I filled the helicopter also, however, helicopters don't possess the same aerodynamic problems as airplanes. Still, I wanted maximum fuel, as I didn't want to run short and have to return to Talkeetna.

"OK, Dave, plan on the biggest bull ride ever. You'll be bucked every way but loose. If either of us gets bucked off, I hope people will remember we did our best. Taxi slowly to the runway. Keep the aileron turned into the wind. Don't back taxi; just take off at the intersection. I know it's short, but with this much wind, you should be airborne in about 100 feet. Keep your airspeed around 110 knots. Make every turn shallow and don't slow down while flying downwind. Never use the flaps." Dave listened intently and nodded as I gave him instructions.

"These kids can't be more than ten miles from Trapper Creek, so start down the west side of the Susitna River at Trapper and fly about ten miles. Move a half-mile west and fly back. Keep moving a half-mile west with each pass. Stay up on the company frequency and keep talking to me. I don't want to meet you in the sky out there. If you get back to the airport in one piece, don't turn off the runway. Keep the propeller in high RPM and wait for the crew to bring out the pickups. Tie one to each wing before trying to taxi to the hangar. Do you think you can do this?"

"Not a chance, DB, but I'll try. If I have any problems, I'll call you on the radio."

"Good luck, Dave. Let's go find them!" We shook on it and headed for our aircraft.

"Talkeetna Radio, this is helicopter 1086 Yankee with Cessna 5311 Uniform. We are a flight of two, we would like a special VFR to depart the area to the west."

"Helicopter 1086 Yankee, have you lost your mind? Nobody can fly in this weather."

"Talkeetna, do you still have a mile visibility?"

"DB, I'm reporting just a mile visibility, and I just recorded a gust over 60. You won't make it off the ground."

"Talkeetna, do you have any reported IFR traffic inbound?"

"No, not at this time."

"Talkeetna, you'd better hurry with my permission for special VFR. Dave is already starting to move and my rotors are turning."

"Helicopter 1086 Yankee and Cessna 5311 Uniform, you are cleared to depart Talkeetna airport traffic to the west. Remain clear of clouds. DB, you're a crazy fool! Good luck."

I watched Dave taxi 5311 Uniform to the runway. The crosswind was so strong the left wheel came off the ground several times, the right wing tip nearly striking the ground. He inched the plane around the corner, and headed into the wind. The engine roared to life. Just like I predicted, the aircraft leaped into the sky in about 100 feet and he disappeared into the blowing snow.

In a couple of minutes, I heard, "86 Yankee, go company frequency."

I dialed 123.45. "Tell me what's happening, Dave."

"I've got about a mile visibility, maybe a little less. I can see straight down with pretty good short vision. I'm coming up on Trapper Creek and starting my first run to the south. I'm going to hug the riverbank. I'm level at about 200 feet. I can't get above that or I'll go IFR."

"OK, Dave. I'm on my way. Keep your lights on. I'll do the same."

Helicopters sometimes have an advantage over airplanes. I spun the blades up to 100% RPM – no taxiing for me. When ready, I quickly pulled pitch to the max, mashed the left pedal, and pushed the cyclic forward standing 86Yankee on her nose. Within the length of the hangar, the airspeed reached 100 knots.

"Talkeetna Radio, Helicopter 1086 Yankee and Cessna 5311 Uniform are clear your airspace."

I found the Susitna River where it connected with Trapper Creek. Rather than fly the same path Dave was flying, I flew the opposite pattern, east to west at tree top height. We never stopped chattering on company frequency and in a few minutes, Carol joined the conversation on the office radio. I had never flown in wind like this before. To say this was a "bull ride" was a huge understatement. At times, the helicopter shook so hard my vision blurred.

We had been airborne about 30 minutes when I found the dog handler. The cold zapped his radio batteries and nobody had heard from him for a couple of hours. He snow shoed southwest, but his dog was nowhere in sight.

"Akland Base, this is 86 Yankee."

"Go ahead, Honey."

"Carol, notify the State Trooper I've found their dog handler. He is moving south to west on snowshoes. He appears to be in good shape and is waving with both hands."

"Where's his dog?" Then I saw something moving; it was the dog, a mile and a half ahead of his handler, and he was on a trail. I had watched lots of animals from the air; this dog was working something - definitely not out for a walk.

"11 Uniform, I've got something. I found the handler, but the dog is way ahead of him. Stay high, move to my location and look for any sign."

"Roger, DB. I'm not far from you now. I'll be overhead in a bit." I couldn't hear Dave overhead, but in a minute or so, saw him pass just above me like a rocket.

"Dave, look for anything – tracks, movement, someone in the snow. Find me something! How's your ride up there?"

"I'm still in one piece. Well, maybe not exactly one piece, but she's still flying."

"5311 Uniform, what are you talking about?"

"DB, I've got something in the snow! It's a thin red line. Come straight south to that small drainage and look on the north side in the small clearing."

Within a few minutes, I saw the red line in the snow. With the sun only two fingers above the horizon, the blizzard thickened, reducing visibility even further.

"Cessna 5311 Uniform, I see the red in the snow. There isn't much daylight left, Dave. Take your bird home. I'll check this out and follow you as soon as I can. Be careful landing, and call Carol so she can have the trucks waiting to help you taxi in."

I turned over the red spot and brought the helicopter to a hover with the nose into the wind. Motionless above the spot, my airspeed still read 50 knots. The down wash from the rotor blades ripped at the snow around the red thing, and then it shot up and away. A red scarf, I could see it clearly now.

Keeping the nose into the wind, I hovered left with no forward motion. In just a few hundred feet, I saw another article of clothing: something blue. Like the scarf, when the rotor down wash tore at the snow, the blue thing came loose from its anchor, blew up, danced a bit under me, and vanished. *Those kids are here. They must be. This must be some sort of SOS that they have left for me to find. But why can't I see them?*

I was over an area of sparse trees and only about 50 feet above the ground. The chopper bucked like a bull, and a ground blizzard whipped the area, swirling around the few trees. It was a fight to keep the chopper from slamming into the ground or a tree. *I can't believe it. There they are!*

The kids leaned against a tree on their knees, facing each other, with the tree trunk between them – but they didn't move. Neither child wore a coat or cap; obviously they had removed most of their outer clothing, I guessed, to leave a trail to help rescuers find their final resting place.

I couldn't land close to where the two bodies huddled, so I elected to attempt a landing a few hundred yards away in the clearing, where I spotted the last piece of clothing. With this much wind, a smooth landing was not an option, so I found a good spot, and slammed the helicopter into the snow, deliberately sinking it up to its belly, with the nose slightly down, all the time hoping not to stick the tail rotor. I tightened down the friction knobs on the cyclic and collective, and left the rotor RPM at 100 %. High RPM reduced the likelihood for the main rotor blades to flex into the tail boom, knock it off, and leave me stranded in the bush.

It was difficult to push open the cockpit door against the wind. When I stepped out onto the cargo rack, the door slammed shut. I checked for cargo tie-down straps, and had several. If I could drag the bodies to the helicopter, I would tie them to the cargo rack. Transporting frozen, contorted bodies in the back of the chopper just wasn't possible.

The snow was waist deep, and I had no snowshoes to aid my efforts. Having retrieved many a body in the past, I struggled toward them with great reluctance, loathing what I was about to recover as daylight dimmed.

About 50 feet from the tree, I could clearly see the two young kids, grasping each other with one hand. I wondered if they were saying goodbye with this gesture. I paused, took a deep breath, and then grabbed the boy by his thin undershirt with a brisk jerk, hoping to separate him from the grip of his sister's frozen hand. He moved and made a weak sound. I was terrified, and wanted to run from the scene. After stepping back a few feet, I came to my senses. He was alive! I hadn't even considered that option moments earlier. His limbs were stiff, but he could move his arm a little. Soft sounds came from his throat. I hurried around the tree to the girl. Her face and limbs were icy cold. I checked her mouth and nose - she was still breathing. Adrenaline surged through my body!

I laid both kids on their backs. The snow was too deep to carry either child, so I gripped the boy by his undershirt, drug him to the helicopter, and ripped open the back door. I forced his frozen body into the back seat, where he kneeled on the floor, facing the seat, with his head on the cushion. I dashed back, faster this time, to the spot where the girl laid, as I now had the makings of a beaten trail. I dragged her in the same manner to the helicopter. She was frozen stiff, so I worked hard to position her in the back seat.

Back in the pilot's seat, I loosened the friction knobs. Deep in the snow, I gently pulled a little pitch and worked the cyclic until the chopper broke free of nature's icy grip. As soon as it felt light, I pulled maximum pitch and rocketed into the sky. Once airborne, I contacted Carol on the company radio.

"Akland base, this is 86 Yankee."

"Go ahead, 86 Yankee. This is Akland base."

"Carol, I have the two kids. They are frozen stiff but still breathing. My visibility is nearly zero. I'm working my way home right at treetop. Call the EMT's and get an ambulance at the airport. I don't have enough fuel to attempt Anchorage."

"The hangar is full of people now. We will get the ball rolling and be waiting for you. Dave arrived some time ago. When we didn't hear from you, we thought you might have gone down."

I could only see straight down. Using the top of the next tree for reference, - and then the next, - the forest slid beneath me. A few minutes later, I found the Susitna River and soon the lights of Talkeetna came into view. I thought it best to land in front of the hangar, where the wind would be better blocked, and started my approach. But when I slowed, the wind became so rough the helicopter bucked, and violently rocked, nearly crashing into the hangar. I pulled all the power she would give me and went around again, making a tight turn over the runway, attempting another try. This time I aimed for an open spot in front of the fuel pumps. The wind blasted, 86 Yankee bucked and bolted, but I got her down. I kept the RPM high and when the helicopter settled, motioned for the EMT's to remove my passengers.

They took the two kids and laid them out on the office floor. Carol was an EMT and worked with the others to cut away frozen clothing that revealed stark white limbs. When Carol thumped on the boy's leg with the scissors, it sounded as though she rapped on a wooden desk with a hammer. I became light headed and nearly collapsed.

"Dave, go pump 30 gallons of jet fuel in 86 Yankee."

"What for, DB? Can't we just shut her down and pull her in the hangar?"

"I wish! There's still a tracker and his dog out there, and he has no idea that we found the kids."

"Geez, DB, do you have a death wish?"

"Give me 30 gallons and make it fast. Check my fuel cap. When it's fastened, give me a thumbs up and get out of the way."

I flew the same track to the site where I had found the kids. If I was lucky, the tracker and his dog would trail them to that spot by the time I arrived. Thirty minutes later, I hovered in, made a couple of turns, and sure enough, there was the tracker with his dog on a leash. *Good work, Guys.*

I landed the helicopter exactly as I had earlier. The exhausted tracker crawled into the back seat and pulled his dog in after him. The animal was so tired his handler had to drag him in. Once onboard, the dog flopped on the floor; both passengers had spent all their energy. The trip back to Talkeetna was slow. In complete darkness, I had to fly with my nose pointing into the wind, hovering from treetop to treetop. With all aircraft lights on, my landing light kept me upright. When the lights at Talkeetna came into view, I set up for another approach to the fuel pump area. I wasn't about to try landing behind the hangar again.

Having learned from my previous experience, this landing went a little smoother. Dave waited with the aircraft tug, and as soon as I touched down, he hooked me up and pulled me to the hangar door. I twisted off the power and pulled hard on the rotor brake to slow the blades. After four revolutions, the blades came to an abrupt stop. The hangar door slid open and in we went, as the doors slid shut. Moments earlier we battled a raging storm, but now we retreated to this heated hangar, everyone too exhausted to talk. The tracker and his dog disappeared without a goodbye.

I sat on the cargo rack for a time. Carol and a couple of other people came out to the hangar, and urged me to come into the office, but I told them I wanted to rest a bit. The truth was my legs shook so badly I couldn't stand.

***

The ambulance crew gathered up the two frost bitten kids from my office floor only minutes before my second landing. Several EMT personnel accompanied the victims to the recently completed Frost Bite Center at the Anchorage Hospital. Because of the severity of the storm, the routine trip of a couple of hours took the entire night. The body core temperature of the kids was dangerously low. On more than one occasion, one or the other ceased breathing only to be revived by the EMTs on board.

The Frost Bite Center was the finest, most modern facility in Alaska. Upon the two frozen kid's arrival, the hospital realized its first real opportunity to prove its superb capability, and test its new equipment

It would be summer before the last child was released to return home. Six months passed, and except for one less toe, the two kids returned to their family and community. In a few years, the pair matured and left the area. 'Little Bit' continued to live in the community, and I can't recall a time seeing her when she didn't thank me for the gift of her two "young'uns."

Helicopter 1086 Yankee survived the adventure without any visible damage. Cessna 5311 Uniform, however, was not so fortunate. The windshield developed a crack that started at the bottom center and ran to the top. Other cracks spider webbed across the Plexiglas. Had it imploded while in flight, Dave's bush pilot career would have abruptly ended. It took two mechanics three months to replace all the pulled rivets and bent sheet metal.

Spring and summer departed. New snows arrived and would remain until next spring. Dave walked into my office and plopped down in the chair beside my desk.

"So, I hear you're going to receive a life saving award for that rescue. I hear that both Senators and the Governor will be there. I guess I get to sit at the table next to you. I think I'll buy a suit. I've never owned a suit."

"I want you to enjoy this special event, Dave, but I'm not going."

"Why not, DB?"

"What we did out there, Dave, was just another day's work. The favorable results were the efforts of many people, not just me. I haven't forgotten that you were there, but they probably won't even mention your name. We still don't know the tracker's name. Doubt they'll mention the EMTs, or the people at the Frost Bite Center either. How about the ambulance driver, and the snowplow operator who plowed ahead of the ambulance for five hours?

This banquet is another political rally. They want me to be one of several dog and pony acts. I told the organizer to send me the award in the mail—it's only a piece of paper. My true reward is that we are both still alive. Hopefully, we'll both get to fly another rescue one day."

Russian Mike

In the Alaskan Bush, moose meat is a winter essential, as vital as firewood and long johns. My family required at least three moose a winter, ten cords of firewood, and I personally preferred one-piece long johns with a trap door - red when I could find them. At minus 40 degrees, the less exposed skin and the quicker you complete body functions, the better. Things can frostbite if you dawdle.

Moose season starts mid-August and runs until spring. Hunters from the lower 48 hunt in the early fall, floating down rivers or trudging through the bush looking for their trophies. They slap at mosquitoes and scratch at "no-see-um" bites. If this isn't irritation enough, Mother Nature often sends them a cold drizzle that lasts for days. I'm sure the more difficult the hunt, the larger the moose becomes, as each story unravels from these hunters upon their return home.

When the first snows arrive, these sportsmen leave for warmer chases. Although I do not hunt for sport, I promised moose hunts to more than a dozen locals in exchange for various favors. For me, hunting is a necessity, spawned from a bad habit: I like to eat!

Around the first of November I switch my Super Cub from wheels to skis. The lakes and swamps are frozen, with about two feet of soft snow cover, and the animals that roamed the high country weeks earlier, staying away from the mosquitoes and hunters, begin to move down to feed on the willows in my area. I like hunting about 65 miles west of Talkeetna, near the upper Yetna River. Each winter this area fills with moose, and there are countless frozen small lakes and swamps on which I can land my agile Super Cub, giving me easy access to my prey.

This year, hunting season began November 16th, the skies sprawled deep blue with occasional white floaters. The temperature couldn't decide which side of zero it wanted to rest on, but either side was fine with me; I needed fresh moose meat.

I lived next to the runway and kept my plane parked beside my house. It was easy to run an extension cord from the house to the electric heater inside the engine cowling. I always kept the engine warm during the winter. Everything I required for the hunt was in my plane, except my faithful Sako 243.

I opened the door and threw the rifle in the back, along with my backpack containing the shells, a meat saw, and lots of nylon cord for tying chunks of moose to the wing struts. The survival equipment was cached in a special compartment behind the back seat.

After removing the engine cover, I pulled the propeller through a few compression strokes, slid onto the seat, gave her four short prime shots, and flipped the magneto switches to both. A push on the starter button and the engine sputtered a few turns and smoothed to a purr. When the oil temperature started to rise, I was ready to hunt.

I ran the power up and pushed the stick forward and back rapidly, bouncing the tail on the snow to break the skis loose from the frozen parking pad. When the plane started to slide, I added a little more power, applied left rudder and turned down the runway. With the throttle pushed to full power, two seconds later I was airborne, watching the frozen Susitna River slide into the distance beneath me.

With the engine roaring and the propeller beating the air into submission, the cockpit was a torrent of noise, but I ignored the sounds and relaxed. I loved flying over the Alaskan wilderness. The ermine carpet below me, dotted with dark green vegetation, was occasionally interrupted by sheer mountains, rising treeless, their stark colors a vivid contrast to the glistening white floor, their craggy walls too steep to allow snow to settle on them. Veins of red and brown among the jagged gray rocks added colorful accents. I floated above a few drainages, and in less than an hour, found my favorite hunting area.

The upper Yetna River is a wide valley with tall mountains on both sides. Moose are plentiful in this area, but I was looking for just the right animal, in the best location. I wanted a large bull moose in an open area where I could easily land, swing the door open and shoot my staple.

After searching for a short time, I spotted a mammoth moose feeding on willows on the north end of a small lake. I made a wide circle around him, setting up for a landing in his direction at the opposite end of the lake. The skis gently settled into the deep fresh snow as the plane slid about half way across the clearing. When I was roughly 500 yards from my prey, I leaned the mixture to kill the engine, and before the plane stopped, applied full left rudder.

The Super Cub had a split door; the top half opened separately from the bottom, and fastened in that position. The way the plane was situated, I could pop open the top door and look under my right wing. The bull continued feeding on the willows, oblivious to my landing, so I unlatched the bottom half of the door and stepped out into the snow. Unhurried, I pulled my rifle from the back seat, chambered a round, and placed the crosshair on his head - a 500-yard shot.

With my target at that distance, the crosshairs inched up with each beat of my heart. I took a deep breath and held it, but couldn't stop my heart from beating, so I allowed the sight to rise above the target and then gently squeezed. A single boom interrupted the silence. I replaced my Sako in the back seat without ejecting the spent round. That critter was either dinner or gone. Either way, I wouldn't be using the rifle again today.

I started 84 Bravo and taxied to the line of willows, where I spied my family's winter meat supply lying on the snow. The moose had not budged from the spot on which he stood when the bullet slammed into his head. It's not possible to load an entire moose aboard a Super Cub, so I field dressed the animal and placed the choice pieces of meat inside the plane. *Next year, a tourist would purchase this trophy rack and help pay for the flying costs of this hunting trip.* Though not a trophy hunter, I knew what this rack was worth. I tied the rack, a real prize, on one wing strut. It measured 72 inches and appeared perfectly symmetrical.

I tied a front shoulder to the other strut, and wrapped the balance of the meat inside the hide. Using my snowshoes as shovels, I covered the hide with about three feet of snow. I hoped my actions would protect the meat until I returned.

The trip back to Talkeetna was just as beautiful as the flight over; except the shadows were longer as the sun on the south horizon started to disappear. A person who lives in the bush feels a real sense of satisfaction bringing home meat, a kind of connection to the land he lives on, but also a sense that he can survive in this inhospitable country. I felt eight feet tall.

Upon my arrival, Carol greeted me with joy, eager to help me park the plane and unload our provision. We would butcher the meat together; actually, Carol did most of the butchering. She loved preparing food for the winter store as much as I loved bringing it home. In a few days, I would retrieve the balance of the moose to process.

I cleaned and prepared the plane for my next flight, knowing my return load would be heavy, and fueled the tank to half full to cut down on the overall weight. I wouldn't need my Sako either, so I left it behind with some survival gear I could do without.

The sky was thin overcast, with a temperature well below zero when I departed exactly as I had two days earlier. There was one difference: I was over confidant this trip. I had not checked the weather forecast, an oversight an old pro like me should never make, but it was only a quick trip out and back.

The overcast thickened by the time I arrived at the location where I had hidden the moose carcass. I dug out the frozen meat and filled my plane with all it could hold and tied the balance to each wing strut. I paid no attention to the changing skies as my plane lifted off the snow covered lake, and turned towards home.

I had flown only a few miles when I realized weather conditions were deteriorating. But I was a well-seasoned bush pilot and thought a little "skud-running" would be good practice, so I climbed to just above the treetops. Conditions looked a little better to the south, so I banked that way, and found a drainage heading in my intended direction. I dropped below the tree line and planned to follow the drainage until it led me to improved weather or the Susitna River, which I could follow back to the house in all but the absolute worst conditions.

I began to encounter ice fog, which consists of super-cooled water droplets suspended in the air, unfrozen until they come in contact with an object. A small amount of glare ice formed on the windshield and obscured my vision, but the defroster burned it away, providing a small hole for visibility just above the dash. Ice also built up on all the other aircraft surfaces. Because glare ice is smooth, it doesn't destroy the wings' lifting ability, but it does add to the aircraft's total weight.

I flew down one drainage, down another, and another, working my way south and east. The weather now captured my full attention. Ice accumulated at a rapid rate. I opened the side window a little for better visibility, as the defroster could no longer keep up. I was still flying, but had to use full power to maintain altitude.

To make matters worse, I wasn't sure of my position. I hadn't seen a recognizable landmark for some time. With my side window slid full back, and my head partly out the window, I tried to steal glances of the scenery below until all visibility vanished. In addition, the Pitot system iced over, causing the altimeter and airspeed indicators to fail.

All options were exhausted. I hoped my wings remained level. With available engine power maxed out, and no functioning flight instruments, I waited for Paradise and imagined heaven. The fear I felt earlier had been replaced by a strange calm. I accepted my fate and waited to see Jesus.

I relaxed my grip on the stick and allowed the plane to soar free. The engine groaned under its load, but the plane kept flying and flying. I began to think that, perhaps, I had already died, and this was an after-life dream of absolute whiteness when the plane slammed hard onto a frozen lake.

My head snapped forward and smashed into the dashboard as my ice-covered plane bounced back into the air and flew a few hundred feet. I chopped the power and pulled the mixture knob. In a few moments, the Super Cub hit the ice again. The propeller stopped turning before the plane settled into the snow. I sat in total silence, a quiet made all the more poignant by the absence of the small engine's roar. I touched body parts: Nothing missing, broken, or bleeding.

I sat silently for a long time, still unconvinced I had survived the landing, but finally came to my senses. I had to prepare for a night in the bush. I had a sleeping bag, and could crawl into it and spend the night in the pilot's seat. I unrolled the bag and threw it on the front seat floor, then crawled into the cockpit after it and began working myself into place for a cold miserable night.

"You want help?" Startled, I looked up. An old man had appeared out of nowhere. He was short and gaunt, and dressed in woolen clothing from his head to his knees, with moose mukluks protecting his feet from the harsh cold.

"Where did you come from? Can you tell me where I am? Do you live near here?" I wanted answers now!

The old man offered no response. He stuck his head inside my door, evaluating my sleeping arrangements. "You come with me. I live over there. My cabin near, by the trees. You be warmer there."

He didn't wait for me, turned away and started walking off. I hurriedly pulled myself out of the seat and struggled to exit the plane. My mummy-style sleeping bag hung around my waist and tangled at my feet. I slid out the door and landed on the snow next to my right ski, then kicked off the sleeping bag, grabbed it, and hurried after the stranger. In the poor visibility, I had trouble keeping him in sight. On top of that, my legs were still weak from the earlier scare, so my first few steps were shaky. But I gathered some inner strength, and before the old guy reached tree line I caught up with him. His cabin stood just beyond the trees that marked the lake's shore, where the ice pushed up against the earth.

He motioned me inside and pointed to his bed. The cabin was a small, containing a bed, a small wood cook stove, and a table and chair. Every available inch was filled with newspapers, magazines, and calendars.

"What your name? I, Mike. I from Russia. No man come here before. You much welcome. I make tea. You rest now."

As soon as the water started boiling in the old coffee can, Mike put in a handful of birch bark, allowed it to steep for a spell and then added a pinch of green spruce needles. He opened the cabin door, filled his hand with fresh snow, and sprinkled it over the steaming brew.

"What are you making, Mike? Is this drinkable?"

"I make Siberian tea. You will like. Tea needs to sit longer. No hurry now. You rest."

"Why did you put snow in the tea?"

"First make tea. When ready, add snow or cold water. Things that float go to bottom."

I was ready for anything hot, but it was obvious that Mike couldn't be hurried. While the steaming tea rested, Mike opened the small oven door revealing a pot simmering inside. He sat the pot on top of the stove and removed the lid. Mike had been boiling a spruce hen for supper. It looked as if the whole bird was jammed into the pot. The head, beak, and feet were all there. After closer inspection, I discovered a few feathers floating as well.

He divided the cooked bird equally between us, placing my half in a large bowl while he ate his portion from the pot. The boiled spruce hen was all he had to offer, but he gave me the choice parts. I was happy he kept the head and feet for himself. Except for the bones and the odd feather, I ate everything in my bowl. When I saw Mike drink the last bit of liquid from the pot, I did the same. Then, he cracked open the head and sucked out the brains, and did the same with each eyeball. I stared as he pried open the beak and pulled out the tongue, happy he had given me the better parts.

After our meager meal, Mike attended to the dirty dishes by opening the cabin door, stepping out into the cold night air, and dropping the dishes in the snow. He rubbed snow on each piece until it was as clean as possible, and then placed them back on the small table. He stepped outside again, returned with an armful of firewood, filled the wood cook stove with all the fuel it would hold, and then placed the balance near the oven.

Considering there was only one small bed in the cabin, I would have been happy to sleep on the floor, but Mike wouldn't have it that way. He pulled back an old wool blanket with lots of holes, and tried to fluff the hard, dried moss stuffed mattress. On top, Mike placed three caribou hides. The first to go to bed, I crawled into my sleeping bag and wiggled against the wall. Mike stacked several more hides on the end of the bed, then laid down next to me and pulled the hides, one at a time, over both of us. Under any other circumstances, I wouldn't have accepted the sleeping arrangements, but tonight I didn't give the situation a second thought. Before he completed arranging the hides, I was fast asleep.

Sunlight filtered through the small pane of glass that served as the cabin's only window when I became aware of my surroundings. Mike must have been up for some time. The cook stove heated, and more birch bark tea was brewing. Bread that looked like a flat biscuit, cooked in a skillet on top of the stove. I worked my way out of my sleeping bag and sat on the edge of the bed. Mike put two biscuits in the same bowl I used the previous night. In the bottom was a pile of yellow-looking lard.

"What's this yellow stuff, Mike?"

"Bear fat I cook down. Real good, make you ready for today."

I shoved my biscuit in my mouth and gave it a try. Bear lard tastes foul, but what the heck! As long as the tea held out, I could wash anything down. With breakfast over, Mike washed the dishes exactly as he had the previous night, and placed them on the table again.

I was ready to face my plane, so Mike and I walked back to where my flying block of ice had come to rest the night before. The sun burned through a thin overcast and the ice fog was gone. It seemed incredible to me that I made it this far, carrying so much ice. The wings and horizontal tail feathers had nearly two inches frozen on the leading edges. The antenna wire that ran from the top of the cockpit to the top of the rudder was encased with ice. The windshield had an inch layer at the bottom, and two inches of ice toward the top. Little wonder the defroster couldn't keep it clear. Even the propeller bore a thick gleaming crust.

"How did this little angel keep flying?" I asked aloud. Mike just scratched his head and smiled, maybe at my angelic reference to my plane.

I carried a small Coleman one-burner stove in the storage compartment behind the back seat, next to a short piece of six-inch stovepipe. I lit the stove, and when it was ready, slid it under the engine cowling and placed the stovepipe on top of it, funneling heat to the back of the engine.

I found a twenty-foot piece of rope in the same compartment. Over the years I had learned lots of uses for rope. Today, this rope would remove the ice from the aircraft surfaces. When the ice was removed, I could fly again - if I could get her started - no sure thing. I threw the rope over the left wing and pulled it underneath, standing back about six feet. Mike held one end of the rope and I held the other. With a sawing action we pulled it back and forth, rubbing at the wing's surface. With each repetition, a little ice wore away. When we grew tired of this, we would tap on the landing gear legs or an antenna, chipping away some of the frozen crystals.

"You much moose here," Mike commented.

"Mike, would you like to take some of this moose back to the cabin and fix it for dinner?" I should have thought of this sooner. I wasn't looking forward to boiled spruce hen again, and definitely sure that Mike couldn't make enough birch bark tea to wash down any more bear fat.

"Mike, I saw a toboggan at your cabin. Go get it, and take some moose home. If I'm to get this plane flying again, I'll need her to be a little lighter for take off anyway."

Without a word, Mike started for the cabin, and in a few minutes I saw him reemerge from the tree line with the toboggan in tow. I continued sawing on the ice-covered wing with my rope-pulling method, while Mike removed moose meat from both wing struts. He stacked the frozen chunks on his sled, then went to the door of the plane and started removing more from the inside of the cockpit. The toboggan was now stacked with meat.

Mike asked, "You want me make dinner?"

I was really hoping he would fix moose. "Sure, please do. I can handle this." Off he went.

The one-burner heater worked fine; the engine warmed nicely, and the heat had removed most of the ice from the windshield. Several hours later, I still worked to remove ice from the plane, but the temperature was dropping. It was time to quit. I turned off the heater, and stowed it and the stovepipe in the back seat. The engine felt warm enough to start, so I prepared to try. Standing behind the propeller, I gave it a good swing. Without a sputter, the engine came alive. I crawled inside the cockpit to stay clear of the prop blast, ran the motor up and let it heat up. After about twenty minutes, the aircraft engine had warmed completely, so I shut it off and slipped from the cockpit into the black night. I turned the propeller by hand so it covered the engine bug eyes, pleased to see that the ice was nearly gone from the propeller. Air friction against the turning prop had removed the ice from the tips, leaving a small area of white near the hub. The overcast sky departed, leaving behind a star-filled sky, whirling overhead. My bush pilot forecast predicted clear skies tomorrow. I could go home.

I smelled moose cooking as I walked back. At the cabin, I gazed upon a "near" feast. Mike had cooked lots of moose: moose simmered in a skillet and moose baked in the oven. A stack of those flat biscuits beckoned from the table sitting next to a cup filled with a red sauce that turned out to be rose hip butter. Most of the seeds were removed, but without sugar it tasted tart, still immensely better than bear fat.

There had been no lunch, and the previous dinner and breakfast were meager, to say the least.

"This is a real feast!" I said as Mike slowly served the portions, and repeatedly placed small servings in my bowl. When neither of us could hold any more, he washed the dishes and tidied up a bit.

I sat on the edge of the bed to let my huge meal digest while Mike leaned back on the only chair. He looked at me and then glanced away, and looked at me again, as if thinking hard about something he wanted to share with me.

Finally, he said, "I from Russia. I live in Alaska nineteen years and a little more. You first person ever here. It make me happy you come."

Mike's English was broken, but I was able to comprehend his story. He wanted me to know about his life, and how he had come to live in this small cabin for more than nineteen years. He began slowly, the emotion in his face told me of sad experiences.

At the end of World War II, Mike explained, he wasn't yet thirty years old. He had fought in the war, and after the battles were over, found a job teaching school in St. Petersburg. He taught college-level classes and became active in politics, believing that Russia would become a free country similar to that of the United States. He read everything he could find about America, and inquired about coming here to teach, or do other work. Mike said he had attended a few rallies, and believed that his political involvement targeted him for collection. Late one evening, he was picked up at his apartment by policemen and held without a charge for several months in a local prison. When he was finally given a trial, his sentence numbed him. He was sent to a Siberian labor camp for ten years, for crimes against the state. He knew this was a death sentence. Few men returned from Siberia after ten years. He had not plotted against Russia, nor committed any crime, but in Russia, to be charged was sufficient, and there was no appeal process.

A few days later, a truck came to transport him to prison. In the back were other men, also sentenced to hard time in Siberia. The truck made stops along the way, picking up other convicted people. Mike told me he arrived in Siberia in early fall, when the colors of the surrounding forest were beautiful. The labor camp was in a remote area, which is Siberia by definition: wilderness surrounded by more wilderness. He was lucky to meet some men who taught him how to survive in the concentration camp. His captors made him work ten to twelve hours a day with few provisions, poor shelter, and sparse clothing. He said it was lucky for him the weather was mild those first few months, allowing him time to prepare for winter mentally, while his comrades taught him to stash anything that could be used during the cold months ahead. Mike was fortunate to find some short pieces of string and wire, plus a long-term prisoner who showed him how to snare small game using these items. At first, Mike caught nothing, but after many tries, he made his first catch: a rat, which he shared with his comrades.

Mike lived in shabby barracks with seven other men, three of them arrived with him, the other four had been incarcerated for years. The walls of the building were thin, with occasional cracks here and there. Precious little sunshine seeped in through one small window to the right of the door. The building had one other source of light, a dim bulb suspended from a wire above a table. A wood or coal-burning potbelly stove provided little heat. Food was delivered each evening in a round pot with a sealed lid, the ration for all eight men. They learned to portion it out, some for the evening meal and the balance for breakfast.

Mike said he skinned and quartered that first rat, placed it in the pot with the food ration, and disposed of the entrails and skin in the stove. It wasn't much, but any extra sustenance would help them survive. Encouraged by his first catch, Mike secretly set a few snares in the fields where he worked. In a few days, he caught a Siberian hare, which are good-sized, and a real prize. If he had been caught with the rabbit, he would have been severely disciplined. He told me he loosened his trousers and slipped the catch inside, positioning it in such a way that it would remain against his crotch. Later that night, he skinned the animal, but this time everything went in the ration pot, even the intestines, which he stripped, and then the droppings. After all, it was only grass and water mixed together, he related, and smiled at my grimace. The skin was saved and later dried. Late that night, the eight men in Mike's barracks swore an oath to never reveal his developing talent.

Winters in Siberia are long and brutal. Each man had his own bunk, but often the men received no fuel to warm their nights. On those occasions, they would sleep two to a bunk, and at times, all eight men slept huddled together to keep from freezing. They kept track of the time with the light bulb, which was turned on and off by the guards. When it came on, it was time to rise, and when it went out, it was time to sleep. To entertain themselves, they told stories of how life was before Siberia. After a few years, someone in the group told a story of how life would be after he was released. This was a wonderful thought, so Mike began to tell stories of what he would do when he returned to St. Petersburg.

Four years slipped away, and Mike said he snared small game every few days. Usually, it was a rat, but sometimes he captured a rabbit, or a mink. Everything went into the pot except the skin. He kept the hides, dried them, and hid them for future use. To make clothing or a blanket might result in discovery, and all of them would be punished: Mike for his skills, and the others for not reporting his activities.

It was about this time that bad news came, Mike said. One of the eight was scheduled for release. Mike had often told stories of what he would do when he could go home. This day, his companion was told his time would be extended for no reason. Bitter with disappointment for his friend, and because he knew the authorities would probably keep them all there until they died, that night Mike told his first story about escaping.

As cold replaced the heat from the potbellied stove, the eight men made another oath. *They would escape.* It was common knowledge throughout the camp that few men ever left alive. They had no way of knowing if anybody had ever escaped. But the men pledged to try, even if it meant dying in the process. There were no more stories at night. They talked of nothing but escape.

In time the eight comrades realized they were doing better than the other barracks. None of their members had died or been seriously sick, whereas the death rate in the barracks of the other inmates was extremely high. The animals Mike had trapped increased the protein in their diets, and the skins he dried were used as liners in their trousers. By now, Mike had more than twenty snares made of wire or string, along with two needles and some thread.

Six years had passed since Mike first came to the camp, and their plan was to escape in late February. This would allow them time to travel over the frozen ground. If they waited until spring, the water-filled muskegs would stop them from moving quickly to escape any pursuers. Mike, now a skilled trapper, retrieved an animal nearly every day, and the eight men had enough meat to dry some, and store it for their journey. They even bartered dried meat for items they would need for the trip. This was dangerous because they never knew which inmates they could trust, but there were few other choices. To keep suspicions to a minimum, they bartered a little with many different inmates. They traded for little things here and there, careful not to arouse curiosity.

When the day was chosen, the eight were ready. They had fashioned two knives out of scrap metal discovered over the years, wearing out many a stone to sharpen the tools. They also sewed the furs they possessed inside their clothes, and tucked the dried meat in between the layers of fur and clothing. When the morning hour arrived, they walked to the forest where they had been working and assumed their assigned tasks.

When darkness enveloped the forest that night, Mike said the signal that ended their workday was sounded, and the eight comrades deliberately lagged behind the other workers heading for camp. One of the stragglers whispered, "I can't do this. I've lost my nerve." A critical decision had to be made in less than a minute as they neared the point in their trek to camp where they had to make their move or miss this chance to escape. Four comrades decided to flee, and the others decided to return to camp to face whatever consequences fell to them. Mike had the snares hidden on his body. As they departed, the friends who decided to remain in camp gave him the other knife. Mike said he didn't look back, but determinedly fled toward freedom.

Being a geography teacher proved of great value. Mike had prepared for this moment for the past two years. The four men avoided any location where people congregate, because few cities and towns in this part of the world were safe for fugitives. They traveled northeast and lived off the land. Occasionally they came upon native people who knew little of modern civilization. Though unable to understand the Russian language, these people were kind to the comrades and gave them what they could spare.

Mike said that after many trials, enduring hunger and cold, and after much help along the way, more than a year had slipped by when three of four comrades arrived on the east coast of Siberia. One unlucky traveler lost his life to the ravages of winter.

The shore had large piles of driftwood, which they used to build temporary shelter. Birds and small game were plentiful; snaring animals and gathering eggs became easy for the first time since Mike had learned this skill. At times, a fish could be caught during low tide.

"If the world not round," Mike told his companions, remembering his old dream of going to America, "I able to see Alaska." Mike knew his escape wouldn't be realized until he arrived in America.

Summer was kind to the three men. They moved north along the shore when their endurance would allow. They would travel for a week or more, and then reestablish a temporary camp to renew their strength. When they were all able, they moved again.

Mike said the days were shortening when nomadic Eskimos discovered them. The two groups were suspicious of each other at first, but soon the Eskimos accepted the white strangers who had invaded their land. The language barrier made communication difficult, but with persistence and patience, the bedraggled travelers in rags, patched together with bits of fur, made their desires known. These native people were seal hunters, and their seal skin boats were a welcome sight to Mike. He had studied the people of the North while teaching at the university, and knew that Eskimos didn't distinguish the land of Russia from that of Alaska. They had family on both sides of the "straits" and hunted both sides, as they willed.

After a short time on the sea, the three refugees joined a sealskin flotilla crew paddling into the bay of Shishmaref, Alaska. They were truly free. Winter threatened the North Country, so when the three outsiders were encouraged to spend the dark months with the "people," they gratefully accepted. Eskimos welcomed the new blood into their families.

Shishmaref was an ancient Eskimo-whaling village, Mike told me. The native homes were dug into the ground, their roofs made of whale ribs covered with sealskins, and a layer of moss mixed with dirt. The only structures above ground were the missionary's home, the church, and the trading post managed by a white man.

Mike became friends with the missionaries and worked on his English daily at home, as he sipped tea. He found he could read English much better than he could speak it, and collected everything he could find written in English. In a short time, he communicated haltingly in English, much the same as he now talked to me.

The missionary wrote letters to the main church office in Anchorage telling them of the three Russian refugees who lived among the native people. The church considered it their responsibility to inform the State Troopers of these foreigners.

As spring arrived in the North, Mike often spent his time at the trading post, where the manager operated the only radio in the community. Mike was present one day when he heard a radio communication that related information about a State Trooper in route to Shishmaref to check out the three Russians. He feared being deported, so that afternoon he met with the other two escapees and discussed their options. That evening, Mike and one other man slipped out of Shishmaref unnoticed. The third member of the group decided to remain and face the consequences because he had taken a woman among the people and would be a father in a few months. Mike never learned of his fate, and related this phase of this story with obvious sadness.

The two refugees returned to the bush and continued their trek toward Anchorage. More than a month later, they arrived in Galena, Alaska, where they decided to rest, using the time to gather their strength, and some supplies. They had hoped to remain in Galena, but the people in this land were Indians, with unfamiliar ways.

Mike and his comrade realized it was time to go their separate ways. Since leaving Shishmaref, they hadn't agreed on much, and in times of despair, his comrade talked about returning. Mike was opposed to that idea, more afraid of being returned to Siberia than of death in the wild.

A few days later Mike was on his own, pushing toward Anchorage, hoping to settle where he knew a large community of Russians lived. The comrades bid no farewells. They had different goals and headed in different directions. As a result of his contact with the missionaries, Mike was now a Baptist but desired to explore his Russian Orthodox faith once more. By midwinter, Mike arrived at the spot where he now lived and related his life's story to me.

Upon his arrival at this remote location, he made camp and began snaring animals, discovering the area rich in wildlife. In a short time, he accumulated a large collection of pelts. While on a trek to Anchorage, he discovered Teeland's Trading Post in Wasilla, Alaska, only two days from his camp. The manager of this small town store gave him fair trade for his pelts, and the people didn't ask questions about his accent, or his tattered clothes. He received his goods and walked back.

The following spring, Mike built the first of three cabins that stood on the property where we sat. As the need arose, Mike would return to Teeland's to trade pelts for the goods he required. With each return from Wasilla, Mike brought back all the printed material he could carry. He cherished newspapers, magazines, and calendars, anything he could find with the written word on it.

Nearly two decades had slipped away. Mike settled into his new home, unnoticed in the small community where he traded. The people of Wasilla knew his face, but no one inquired about his life. The day that Mike invited me to his cabin, I became the first person to ever visit his home in the bush.

There was no way of knowing the hour, but Mike consumed most of the night telling me his story. I crawled back into my sleeping bag and rolled against the wall. I didn't wait for Mike to retire, and was asleep in seconds.

Mike woke me the next morning, aware I had better take advantage of the sunny day to return home. With birch bark tea and a biscuit or two to fill my stomach, I walked through the snow to my plane, and began the process of heating the engine and sawing at the ice with my rope-pulling method. Sunny skies made everything seem warmer. When I tried to start the plane, it popped to life with a roar and settled down to a smooth idle.

I was ready to leave when Mike asked me to come back to the cabin with him once more. I left the plane idling and walked up the beaten path to his home. He took a calendar and pointed to Thanksgiving Day. "I want you and family come for Thanksgiving. I make you fine meal."

"We will come for Thanksgiving. About mid-day," I told him, but didn't intend to keep that promise; it was a kind gesture of goodbye, nothing more.

The engine roared and the tail lifted. Within a couple hundred feet, I was airborne and banked left to the north. Mt. McKinley was in full view. Anytime I could see that mountain, I could find my way home. I flew back over Mike's cabin, waving my wings in goodbye, and an hour later, slid onto my parking pad at the house.

Carol greeted me with her usual collected composure. "I'm glad you decided to come home. The ice fog rolled in here about two hours after you departed. I knew you would be out for a day or two. Did you bring the entire moose home? This doesn't seem like much meat."

"Lovie, I've got a story to tell that you won't believe, but first, help me cover the engine and get the meat out of the plane." As we worked together preparing the plane for its night's rest, I told Carol of my adventures and those that Mike had told me.

Carol listened with keen interest. "I reckon you want something other than spruce hen for dinner."

"I'm hungry enough to eat anything you prepare. What would you think about going to Mike's for Thanksgiving dinner? Hopefully, he will have something other than boiled spruce hen. I left him most of the moose meat I had onboard, and he fixed me a good moose dinner while I was there." I was already beginning to have second thoughts about my accepting his invitation only as a gesture of kindness.

"I was planning to have Thanksgiving at the church like usual, but if you really want to go, we can make it happen. Do you think it's safe to take the boys with us out there? He's not crazy or anything like that, is he?"

"To tell you the truth, Lovie, he's the nicest bush rat I've ever met. I think you'll love him. I know he would really like to meet our boys."

Nine days later, I packed the plane for the trip to Mike's house. A Super Cub is a three passenger aircraft with all the passengers in tandem. The kids were small, so I put both boys in the far aft seat, loaded ice cream and eggs on their laps, and stuffed cans of fruit and jam around them. The kids were packed in so tightly they couldn't move. Carol sat in the middle seat and I loaded bags of flour and sugar in her lap. Between her legs, I stashed the potatoes and yams on the floor. I crawled in the front seat, and once again made a left turn onto the runway and we were airborne. The sky was absolute blue, and the snow below us spangled like fields of glitter.

Even though it had snowed since I was at Mike's lake, I could see the spot where I previously landed. A quick "fly-over" Mike's cabin revealed how well his place was hidden in the trees. If I hadn't known it was there, I would never have seen it. I'm sure he planned it that way, afraid in those early years that discovery might mean deportation.

I made a 180-degree turn and landed to the north, then taxied back to the shoreline, stopping as close to the cabin as I could. I popped open the doors, and spotted Mike standing near the tree line. He didn't move or wave.

"I hope he knows that today is Thanksgiving. Maybe he's had second thoughts about people coming to his home. Lovie, if things don't go smoothly from the get-go, let's put off the food, say howdy, and leave."

"To tell you the truth, Dennis, he looks scared to me. Help me out and I'll go meet him."

As soon as I had the flour off her lap, Carol jumped out and headed up the trail. "Mike, I'm Carol. Thank you for saving my husband's life. We've brought food and goodies. When was the last time you had ice cream?" Carol never knew a stranger.

"I afraid you not come. You welcome here. Come my house." Carol reached out and gave Mike a big hug. His arms remained stiffly at his side. Then he reached around her and embraced her robustly; tears flowed down both cheeks.

Carol trudged up the path to the cabin, while I unloaded the supplies and the two boys. "Cory, there's a toboggan at the cabin door. Run get it, and bring it back to the plane. We'll pull these groceries up to the cabin." Off he went, returning a minute later with the sled. We stacked all the goods on it and pulled them to the door.

I could hear Carol laughing and carrying on long before I got to the house. When I opened the door, I was shocked to see the improvements Mike had made. The place was decorated with festive paper. Everything was neat and in its proper place. The heaps of newspapers were folded and stacked in tall piles - lots of piles.

I hoped for moose meat, and prayed there wouldn't be any boiled spruce hen. When Mike opened his oven door, we were delighted to see a feast in the oven - a turkey, golden-brown and stuffed with apples and oranges, and basted to perfection.

Mike set the pan holding the turkey on the table. "Dennis, you bless food?" I thanked God for this wonderful day. Mike was still a Baptist in his heart.

He carved the meat with his skinning knife and we ate from the pan. There was only one bowl in the house and not enough eating utensils to go around, so we consumed the feast with our fingers, and used our pant legs for napkins.

"Mike, that was the most wonderful turkey I've ever had. How did you get a turkey way out here?"

"Day you leave, I go to town and trade for turkey and supplies. I want to go town anyway. It just short hike for me. I make turkey like when I lived in St. Petersburg. I hope you like."

"Mike, it's a two-day hike to town and two days back. You did that for our Thanksgiving meal?"

"I 72 now, and two days are nothing. I stay gone six days. I stay two days in town. I even had Vodka and brought a little home. We have a wee little before you go."

"Mike, could you show us some of your pelts you use for trading?" I asked.

In the early years, Mike had built three buildings on his home site, each a few feet from the others. As he grew older, he built a covered walkway between the buildings, allowing him to go from shack to shack without going outside. I had been invited into his cabin, but had not seen inside the other structures. He proudly showed us his two work sheds, piled with dried black bear and brown bear hides, and stacked four feet tall. An abundance of mink, martin, beaver and wolf hides reached the ceiling. A stack of eagle hides, with the feathers intact, stood taller than my boys. "Mike, what do you do with the eagle hides?"

"Teeland no longer trade them, so I trade with Indians west from here."

Mike didn't have a dog team; and didn't own a trap. He had snared every one of these critters. We stood among thousands of dollars of hides and furs. If he got caught with these pelts in his possession, he would face prison. This was his retirement plan; he knew nothing of possession limits. For him, this was survival.

We talked until our throats were sore, and laughed until our tummies ached. "Can have ice cream now? I not remember the last time I have ice cream. We have vodka, too."

I filled his only bowl with ice cream, while Mike poured a little vodka in three old canning jars. He ate his ice cream and we sipped vodka with him. The boys sipped birch bark tea, with lots of sugar.

The sun rested one finger above the horizon when we walked to the plane. Mike gave our boys a little hug each, and helped them into the small space in the back of the plane. He gave Carol a big Russian bear hug. "Thank you come to my home." When she turned to climb in the plane, he spun her around and gave her another hug. I too, received a hearty Russian hug.

"You make me happy. Please come back again. I know I miss people. Thank you for first Thanksgiving dinner." Mike's light blue eyes filled with tears, that spilled over and ran down his cheeks.

It's hard to understand a day like this. We flew home without saying a word. When we arrived at our house, Carol couldn't hold it in any longer. "Dennis, how is it possible that Mike knew today was Thanksgiving? If you stop and think about it, he spent six of the last nine days hiking to town and back. I've never had such a wonderful Thanksgiving. What would he have done if we hadn't shown up?"

"Carol, you're talking way too fast. Mike has lots of calendars. He must have marked the days off. I know one thing, I'll never forget this Thanksgiving."

After that special holiday, I landed at Mike's every time I flew close to his area. He enjoyed ice cream, fresh eggs, and the vegetables we supplied him, a special treat to a bush rat who seldom purchased such items. Carol often prepared him care packages of wool socks, mittens, chocolate chip cookies, and a generous supply of candy bars. He quit drinking birch bark tea and started drinking coffee when Carol sent him five pounds of fresh ground coffee with each trip.

After the lake froze in winter, I'd make my first trip on skis to check on Mike. When I purchased my first helicopter, I landed next to his house near shore in a clearing so small the main rotor blade turned inches from the trees, and the tail rotor hung over the water. The risk was well worth my time with Mike.

With each visit, Mike would tell me more stories of his life and adventures. He wanted to be remembered after he left this life, and I promised Mike I would pass on his story once he was gone. He cautioned me, "Don't tell until I gone, or they come and get me."

Several years after our first meeting, I discovered the fate of the Russian who separated from Mike at Galena, Alaska. Unbelievable as it may seem, he found a site very similar to Mike's, and spent more than twenty years on the west bank of the Susitna River, living as Mike had lived. He was known as Crazy Ivan. The two Russians lived out their lives in Alaska only a hundred miles apart, but never saw each other again after their departure at Galena. I tried to get the two of them together for a meeting, but about that time, a BLM helicopter crew discovered Crazy Ivan's cabin. A few days later, he was arrested and deported to the USSR. Mike's caution rang loud in my head.

I never told Mike that his old comrade had been returned to his homeland. Mike was in his late seventies and didn't need that kind of fear haunting him. He had experienced trauma enough for one lifetime, so I kept his very existence a secret, never telling a soul of the friend I flew to visit whenever I got the chance.

I was closing the hangar late one August when I received a phone call from an Alaska State Trooper investigator, who told me A BLM helicopter had found Mike's home site about six weeks earlier. On examination of the cabin, they found Mike's body in his bed. He had died from natural causes, making his final escape to paradise only a few weeks before his home was discovered. It took the investigator about six weeks to complete his work; he found my name among the many papers Mike had hoarded. He left a will of sorts, leaving me everything, but I was advised that, because Mike was an illegal alien, all his possessions were confiscated by the state. Mike's cabins were burned to the ground, and I was warned not to land at the site again. The state donated Mike's body to science.

I miss Russian Mike, but I'm thankful only his body was found. He never had to leave his adopted home except to take that last trip we all must take. I raise my glass of vodka in remembrance and salute.

"Mike, I'm sorry I didn't listen a little longer the last time we were together. Thank you for your friendship. Thank you for sharing your life with me. Now that you are safe, I will tell your story."

Mary's Bear

The Laundromat was frequented more than the Fairview Inn. A beer is nice, but if you are coming in from the bush, the first thing you need is to get in line to wash your clothes. At times, it takes an entire day to complete this task. With about a hundred people living in town, and another hundred living in the bush, the four washing machines at Three Rivers ran continuously. Some people never entered the Fairview; after all, it's a bar. But the Laundromat was used by everyone in the area, except the folks who had a washer in their home. It didn't take long to know everyone who lived in the community, and often the best gossip came from what you saw being washed.

Every newcomer to town eventually discovered the Laundromat, so I wasn't surprised to see her there. The odd thing was her attire. *She must be the last, true hippy,* I thought, as I checked out the pile of clothes she was washing. I'd never seen anyone quite like her, a big lady with an even bigger dress draped over her body, a long, faded, purple paisley-print that nearly reached the top of her combat boots. Red long johns crept from under her dress. Wool socks sprouted from the top of her boots and reached toward her knees, the ones with the red bands at the top. Thick, expensive, heavy-duty wool foot-cover that experienced "bush" people preferred. The three dirty dresses lying on the floor were identical to the one she wore, along with at least six pairs of long johns, and a dozen pairs of socks, all exact copies of what covered her body. *I'll bet picking her daily wardrobe is an easy task.*

"You must be new to town. I know everyone in Talkeetna, but I've never seen you before. I'm Dennis, but everyone calls me DB."

She moved away, and checked me out. "Hi, DB. I'm Mary. You're right. Just arrived this morning. Been on the road a few weeks. Guess I'm due for a complete cleaning."

"Looks like you have your work cut out for you. Are you passing through or here to stay?"

"I read about Talkeetna when I was in California. I picked it over every other town in Alaska. I'm here to stay." She opened the lid of a machine and stuffed in some clothes.

"You've been here since this morning, and already you know you want to stay? I'd go slowly if I were you. This country can be tough on Cheechakos. Do you have anyone to stay with? I hope you realize it's still March outside."

"I've got my tent. I'll be just fine." She turned her back to me and resumed her laundry detail.

"You got guts, lady. Don't freeze up. Spring is a long time away." I figured that with such determination, she'd probably make it, and left her to her toil.

I forgot about Mary until the day I walked down the railroad tracks to the Talkeetna River Bridge. It was a beautiful May morning and the perfume of spring permeated the air. Spring's arrival could be judged by the condition of the river ice, so I decided to check it out. Along the tracks, north of the railroad house were a string of abandoned autos, where I saw Mary crawling out the back of a rusted hulk. It was obvious she just awoke and was heading to the bushes for her morning call when I surprised her. She seemed angry with me.

"What are you doing out here? Spying on me?"

"I'm not spying, Mary. I was just checking the ice flow. It's about time for spring. We'll have leaves in a month or so. I hope you're not living in that junk pile."

"My tent crapped out some time ago. I'm doing just fine living here, thank you very much. Besides, what's it to you where I live, Mr. DB?" She glared at me defiantly.

"Simmer down a little, Mary. I don't care where you live. I'm just glad to see you didn't freeze. You've survived some really nasty weather. You'll make it fine now that spring is nearly here."

As she dashed into the bushes, she yelled back at me. "I didn't mean to snap at you, but you caught me half dressed. I'm never at my best in the morning."

The only thing I could see she was missing was her dress. Everything else was there: the combat boots, the wool socks, and the long johns. I thought she was dressed well enough. I took a couple more steps when the back door of the rusting relic opened again. Out crawled a little boy who appeared to be about three years old. He followed Mary's trail into the bushes, oblivious to me.

"Mary, is this your son?"

"Mind your own business, DB. Don't be spying on me."

I made my way down to the river bridge and watched the ice float by for a time. When I returned, I walked slowly past Mary's car and saw she was gone. *I wonder where that kid came from? I haven't seen him before. No one had mentioned that Mary had a child.*

Spring finally arrived with summer on its heels. It was good to have the long, warm days back. I turned into Talkeetna Grocery and met Mary coming out, with the boy by her side.

"Hey, Mary, I haven't seen you for a while. Are you and your boy getting along okay?"

"Yep, DB, we're doing just fine, thank you very much." She hurried past me, and headed towards the river.

"Dorothy, what do you know about Mary?"

"Except for the fact that she wears the exact same clothes every time she's in here, not much. I think she's a 'sourdough wanna-be.' She probably read too many Jack London books in California and had to see Alaska for herself. She's taken up with Harold, you know."

"Harold, the crazy gold miner? Now I know she's a fruitcake. Do you know where that boy came from? I met her the first day she arrived, and he wasn't with her then."

"You're right, DB. Other people are asking about him, as well. He sticks to her like glue. He must be her son, but she won't talk about him."

"The reason I stopped was to let you know that I put a CB radio in the office at the hangar. I don't know when we'll use it, but everyone is getting one, so I bought one too. I want to thank you for helping the people in the bush get radios. It will be a big help when emergencies arise. You may have to give me lessons on CB talk. I'm not familiar with all this '10-4' and 'good buddy' stuff."

"I wish I could talk you into putting a CB radio in your helicopter, DB. It would come in real handy. You could talk to lots of folks while you're flying."

"I don't have time to jabber when I'm flying, Dorothy. I've got aircraft radios that keep me busy."

Dorothy's insistence about installing CB's in my helicopters bugged me, but her gossip about Mary and Harold rattled me even more. Harold was a young gold miner who came to town a few years earlier, looking to strike it rich. He always worked alone and stayed to himself. It wasn't until I left the grocery store that I remembered at times he slept in an abandoned auto near the railroad tracks. He and Mary had probably crossed paths there. They both were secretive people; they belonged together.

Before this summer, Harold lived in a large tent about half way up Clear Creek. I flew over his place often, and noticed he was building a cabin. A few miles upstream from his camp sat an old mining village that had been deserted for years. Harold was taking boards from some of the old buildings and moving them, one at a time, to his site. Now, it all made sense. The new woman in his life wanted something better than a tent.

The trek from the old mining village to Harold's camp was nearly three miles through the bush. It was hard work dragging those boards to their new home. Three times that summer, I landed my helicopter at his place to check on them. Each time the pile of old boards grew bigger, and each time Mary greeted me in her purple paisley-print dress. Even in summer, she continued to wear her combat boots, wool socks and long johns. She was probably too warm with all those clothes, but mosquitoes couldn't get to body parts that were covered.

The first snows arrived and Harold was still building his cabin. I had never known Harold to work so hard. He usually left his camp in the winter for parts unknown, and returned in early spring to resume mining. This winter, it looked as though he planned to stay. The days were growing shorter; Mary must have been pushing him to complete their new home. The building was only twelve feet by sixteen feet, but displayed Harold's determination to raise a roof over Mary's head before winter.

Just before Christmas I spotted winter smoke settling along the rooftop of their cabin, so I plopped the helicopter in the front yard.

"I wanted to check on you folks and wish you a Merry Christmas. Your cabin looks real nice. I'll bet you'll be nice and warm in there."

"It sure beats a tent. Look, DB, since you're already here, would you mind giving me a free ride to town? I'll walk back home."

"Sure, Harold, get in. After all, it is Christmas." He hadn't paid anything on his account for the last year, but what the heck! I flew him to town and put him off at the hangar. He trudged off toward Fairview Inn. "Have a Merry Christmas, Harold."

"I'll do what I can." Not even a thank you! Harold was always a little short on social graces.

Throughout the winter, I flew over Mary and Harold's little home. Smoke continued to rise from the chimney, hanging above the cabin and a well-used trail that led to the outhouse. I assumed they were alive and well.

Winter's depression always departs in May. This was the warmest second week of May I'd ever seen, like being wrapped in an eiderdown quilt on a winter's night. I was still in bed, enjoying the warm air sneaking through my bedroom window when the phone rang.

"DB, this is Dorothy. I have an emergency! Mary's on the CB radio. She's alone with the boy at her cabin, and a bear is trying to break in. She's scared to death."

"Where's Harold?"

"He left yesterday for Fairbanks. She's really scared. She says that this is a real mean bear. It's tearing at the boards of the cabin as we speak. You'd better hurry. I think this bear means business."

I could hear Mary's frantic voice in the background while Dorothy talked.

"Tell Mary to hang on. I'm on my way, but I can't get there quicker than an hour. Tell her to make lots of noise and bang metal pans together. Maybe she can scare him away. Tell her to stay inside."

"Lovie, get out of bed and go to the hangar. A bear is trying to break into Mary's cabin on Clear Creek. She has a CB radio. She's talking with Dorothy right now. When you get to the hangar, call Mary on the CB. I'll get Ken and meet you at the office in a few minutes. Try to keep Mary calm. If that bear gets into her cabin, she and the kid will be breakfast."

Ken was the wildlife officer who lived next door to my home. I ran across the yard and banged on his door. "Who's out there?" He yelled from his bedroom.

"Ken, a bear is attacking Mary's cabin. She's there with her boy. Get your rifle and meet me at the helicopter. Hurry!"

Carol had already left the house with the pickup truck so I sprinted to the hangar on foot. I removed the tie-downs from the main rotor blades but didn't even bother to climb inside. Instead, I leaned in and pushed the start button. In a couple of seconds, the turbine engine whined. When the blades stabilized in rotation, I ran to the hangar and grabbed my Browning 12-gauge shotgun. This old Browning was modified with an eleven round magazine and an eighteen-inch barrel. Years before, someone named this killer "Eleanor." She sent many a wayward bear to heaven.

I ran back to the helicopter and threw Eleanor in the back seat. At about the same moment, Ken ran across the parking lot with his rifle in hand, and then jumped in the passenger seat. I pulled pitch while he fastened his seatbelt. We shot straight up about a hundred feet;

I made a pedal turn in the climb and dumped the stick forward. The air speed indicator zoomed past 100 knots before we flew a block.

"Akland base, this is 500 Hughie Charlie. Are you on company radio?"

"I've got you loud and clear, Honey. I also have Mary on the CB. She's frantic. The bear is still clawing at her cabin."

"Is she making lots of noise and banging pans?"

"Honey, Mary's making all the noise she can."

Ken and I looked at each other. "I'll tell you, Ken, this sounds like one mean bear. Maybe he's rabid."

"DB, have Carol ask Mary if there's a gun in the cabin."

"Akland base, this is 500 Hughie Charlie. Does Mary have a gun in the cabin?"

About now, I wished I had listened to Dorothy and put a CB radio in the helicopter. All instruction for Mary had to be passed through Carol first on the aircraft radio. Then Carol would relay the message to Mary on the CB. I clicked away at about two miles a minute, but it sounded as though Mary didn't have many minutes left.

"500 Hughie Charlie, Mary has an old gun, but she's never shot a gun in her life."

"Why do people move to the bush and not first learn to take care of themselves? Don't ask her that. Have her describe the gun."

"500 Hughie Charlie, she says the gun has a long barrel and a wood stock."

"That's just great! Now ask her the size of the hole where the bullet comes out."

"Honey, Mary says the hole is about the size of a quarter."

Ken and I agreed that she had a 12-gauge shotgun. "That will do the job, if we can tell her how to use it."

"Good luck," Ken said.

"Okay, Lovie, ask Mary to look for the shells."

"500 Hughie Charlie, Mary found a big box full of shells."

"I copy that, Carol. Tell her to put a shell in the gun, and tell me when she's ready to fire."

"Dennis, Mary is hysterical! The bear has found the window and is scratching at the pane. She opened the gun barrel, but when she put a shell in, it slid completely through and fell out on the floor."

"Carol, talk slowly to her. Force her to concentrate on your instructions—not on the bear. Tell Mary to look in the box and find a larger shell. Then put the shell in and raise the barrel. Point the gun at the bear and pull the trigger."

"500 Hughie Charlie, Mary can't get the gun to fire. The bear is crawling through the window! I think it's too late."

Ken looked at me and said, "The gun may have a hammer. Tell her to pull back the hammer, and try to fire it again."

"Carol, we are still about seven minutes from Mary's cabin. Tell her that if the gun has a hammer, she must pull back the hammer first before she can fire the gun."

"Dennis, I gave Mary the instructions in the blind. She is not responding to my transmissions."

I looked at Ken. He was ghastly pale, and reached back to pick up Eleanor.

"This is going to be a difficult shot, DB. Hover over the cabin. When the bear comes out, I'll kill him."

"Ken, make sure your seatbelt is fastened. When I see the bear, I'll fly sideways into him. Keep the door closed until I'm right on top of him. Push the door open with your foot, and give this monster his ticket home."

"There's the cabin, DB. Can you hover over it?"

I made a quick stop over the cabin, bringing my Hughes helicopter to a hover. The engine roared, and the rotor blades beat the air into a tornado. Spruce needles and dust flew everywhere. Ken was ready to fire when the door opened. Mary walked out of the cabin with the single shot shotgun in her left hand. She held the boy around his waist with her right hand. Tears streamed down her face as she looked up at us.

Mary and the boy appeared to be safe, so Ken and I flew a few circles around the cabin searching for the marauder. I wanted a piece of this guy, but I couldn't find him, so I landed in the clearing in front of the cabin. Ken bailed out and went inside to calm Mary, while I cooled the engine for the suggested two minutes.

When the blades stopped turning, I followed him inside.

The cabin was filled with the stench of spent gunpowder. Mary had figured out how to make that old gun fire. She sat on the bed, with her emotions now under control. The boy stood behind her, with his arms wrapped around her neck. Damage to the inside of the cabin was visible everywhere.

The bear was crawling through the window when Mary figured out how to load the gun and cock the hammer. Her first shot took out part of the floor. She loaded another shell and shot a hole in the door. By now, the bear was long gone, but Mary's battle was just beginning. Harold had four boxes of 12-gauge shells, and Mary had fired every one, blowing silver dollar-sized holes in all the walls. The window was blasted away. The door was full of holes. The ceiling looked like a star-studded night sky. I gave up counting holes, and started counting the spent shells as I gathered them from the floor. Mary shot all one hundred shells. I was standing in a war zone.

"Mary, can we take you back to Talkeetna with us? I don't think you should stay here with all these holes in your cabin."

"I'll be just fine here, DB. You two can leave now. We don't need any more help."

It was time for us to depart. "Ken, have you ever seen such a stubborn, ungrateful woman?"

"I don't think so, DB. She has a real problem with appreciation. If she could have killed that bear, I'd bet you she would have eaten him."

The next day after lunch, I went to the Three Rivers Laundromat to talk to the owner. Mary and the boy were inside. She had just completed their laundry, and was stuffing the purple paisley dresses, the long johns, and wool socks into her extra-large backpack.

"Mary, you're not leaving us, are you?"

"Mind your own business, DB. I don't need you to keep track of me."

I watched her walk out the door and down the street. The boy hung onto her dress as she pulled him along. When she reached the first curve on the edge of town, I saw her turn and stick her thumb in the air. The second vehicle that approached her, stopped. She and the boy got in, disappeared from sight, and were never seen again in Talkeetna.

Gunnysack Gold

Occasionally, I have a great notion. It came to my attention in the spring of 1979 that the community of Egavik, Alaska, experienced difficulty getting its supplies. The barges that brought the goods to the small town began their journey in Seattle during the early summer, and made stops along the coast of Alaska, leaving goods at ports along the way. Egavik is south of Nome and north of Unalakeet, Alaska, inland from the salt water of Norton Sound. The supplies arrived at Egavik in mid-August.

The tide in this area of Alaska rises and falls thirty-six feet, two times each day. At high tide, the barges move close to shore, where large items such as modular homes, autos, and supply containers can be offloaded. When the tide ebbs, the barges move out to the safety of deeper waters. With the return of high tide, the barges move back to the docking areas, where cranes lift the loads to shore.

To help this small community, I developed a method to transport some of the goods using helicopters equipped with a 100-foot steel cable, fastened to the cargo hook on the belly of the aircraft. We assembled as many small loads as possible and then flew to the barge. Bringing the helicopter to a hover, the aircraft would pick up goods weighing around a thousand pounds and then fly back to a site in Egavik. This system, using a long-line sling load required exceptional skill. Few pilots can fly a helicopter at 120 knots while dangling this hundred-foot cable underneath, weaving the line among the rigging of the barge without becoming entangled. After hooking the rigged box of goods, the heavy helicopter had to fly clear of the vessel, plus any obstacles in the path of the load.

I used two Hiller Soloy helicopters for the two and a half mile flight from the barge to town. On a good day, we could make a round trip in three to four minutes. It took three weeks to off-load the barges that arrived in Egavik during August 1979. When the load weights were totaled, we had transported more than two million pounds of goods from the sea to shore with two small helicopters. This off-loading method became a maritime record. Soon this system was adopted as standard procedure for off-loading barges and ships along the coasts of Alaska, where deep ports had not been developed.

Toward the end of our three-week operation, one of the helicopters developed a vibration in the tail rotor. It was discovered that the main bearing would have to be replaced. It was an overcast day with intermittent light rain; gray skies promised a nasty day. The flight crew and ground crew begged for a rest. I recognized that fatigue was overtaking us and consented to give the crew two days off, while I arranged to have the spare part flown to Nome on Wien Air Alaska's 737. That afternoon I set out for Nome in the functioning Hiller to retrieve the bearing.

"Okay, Bobby, I know your guys will be out partying the minute I disappear from sight. I have an account set up at the restaurant. You can charge your drinks to me. If you buy drinks for anyone else and put it on my tab, you're dead meat. I'll be back tomorrow afternoon. It's your responsibility to have the pilots sober and ready to fly when I return."

Bobby was Chief of Maintenance. I could trust him to keep his feet on the ground, but the pilots were a flaky lot. They could teach sailors on liberty how to frolic.

Visibility was about three miles. Nome was north. All I had to do was follow the black shoreline. On days like this, two colors are noticeable: The sea, land, and sky are gray, and the shoreline black. My simple task was to follow the black line to Nome.

About 30 to 45 minutes into my flight, I came upon an unusual ravine that ran from the shore back into the hills. I had seen other gullies like this, but for some reason, I was drawn to follow the path of this one. I concluded if the drainage kept turning northwest, I would pop out over a few hills and arrive in Nome. If it turned east, I would retrace my path and continue to follow the shoreline. Perhaps I was becoming bored with the gray and black. In truth, I simply felt the urge to check it out.

I quickly considered my options. *I wish I had a map of this area. But I don't really need a map. I'll keep the water on my left side and before the fuel is gone, I'll be back at the Board of Trade, tossing down a cold one.*

I had hours of fuel on board, having topped off the fuel tank, plus ten five-gallon gas cans strapped to the cargo racks. I wanted to explore, and since fuel would not be a problem, I followed the gully due north a short distance, and turned left.

Good guess, I thought. The earthen trench broadened and then narrowed, but after a bit, I became disoriented, not certain which direction I was flying. I turned down a brush-filled creek, having second thoughts about my adventure.

Would you look at that! There's an abandoned mining camp. The visibility was still about three miles, and rain globs hung to my bubble. Even with blurred vision, it was obvious I had discovered a mining settlement, apparently abandoned many years ago.

I should trust my instincts more often. This place is incredible. There were seven buildings. The roofs were collapsed, and creek brush grew through the shingles and out the windows and doors. I made two quick turns over the deserted settlement and landed in the middle of the old camp. *Why is it I forget my camera each time I happen upon a special site like this?*

I stepped out of the aircraft into the light drizzle, and was transported back half a century. I could imagine this site fifty years earlier—men working sixteen hours a day to fill their pokes with gold. *They must have mined it dry and moved out.* I explored the exterior of two old cabins. *I wish I could have seen inside before the roofs caved in. I bet there's some great old stuff under all the rubble.*

I moved on to explore the third cabin, and stepped on something that gave way under my weight. It felt unfamiliar and I was curious about what I had stumbled upon. I found a short piece of board from the cabin roof and clawed at the debris. I could clearly see a rusted metal piece, and was shocked at my discovery!

I had stepped on an old Oneida New House No.6 bear trap. The jaws of the trap were massive, armed with a row of wicked steel teeth on each side. After fifty years, the trap sat ready, patiently waiting for its prey. Had my gait been twelve inches longer, the trap would have slammed shut on my leg, and I would have spent my remaining days at this old mining camp. I carefully uncovered the ancient mammal mine. A half century earlier, it had been tethered to the cabin wall with a short rope, now rotted away except for a knot at the trap and another at the wall.

I pushed the stick against the pan, and the trap that guarded this old cabin crashed shut, snapping the stick off at the jaws. I shivered. *That could have been my leg. I think it's time to head to Nome while I still have all my limbs.* A cold beer at the Board of Trade beckoned. Greedily, I picked up my prize and tied it to the cargo rack. There could be another bear mine hidden close by. I had lost my enthusiasm for exploring.

As I prepared to climb aboard my aluminum steed, I saw a pyramid-shaped pile, taller than the surrounding cabins. It was to the left of the helicopter, less than a hundred feet away. I carefully walked to the pile and scratched at the debris, a dump of sorts. With further examination, I concluded that the miners must have thrown all their trash in this pile. I uncovered glass bottles, old style tin cans, and bones. I noticed that most of the remains in the pile were old rotting gunnysacks. They were completely decayed for the first few inches, but as I dug deeper, I could see more gunnysacks. I had discovered the biggest pile of rotten gunnysacks ever!

With my prize bear trap lashed to the cargo rack, I left the site and made my way to Nome. The sign at the Board of Trade read, "Liquor In the Front, Poker In the Rear." I was in familiar territory. After downing more beers than a man should be allowed to swallow, I found a room next to the bar, and collapsed into bed for some much needed rest.

The next morning after several cups of black coffee and a few aspirins, the effects of too many beers wore off. I picked up the helicopter part from the Wien Air Alaska Office and returned to Egavick. I never gave the old mining site a second thought, but I treasured that bear trap. It was an envied trophy that I would display proudly in my office for years to come.

Bob Young was Talkeetna's most successful gold miner. He often came by my office to chat, and over the years became a trusted friend. In March of 1983, when it was too early in the season to do anything but drink coffee and swap stories, he dropped by for a cup.

"DB, I don't think you've ever told me how you came to own that old bear trap."

"Bob, I've told you that story every year for the last three or four years. I found it near Nome, at an abandoned mining site.

"Yeh, I remember the story. Do you think I believe that tale?"

"It's the truth, Bob. Except for the huge pile of gunnysacks, everything was rotted away. I found nothing worth taking except this old trap."

"Gunnysacks? I don't remember you mentioning that before."

"I may not have mentioned it. Guess it didn't seem important, just an old pile of rotting gunnysacks, pyramid-shaped and as large as a house. There were old bottles, cans and some bones mixed in. Probably the miner's dump site, I figure."

"DB, do you have any idea what those old miners used those gunnysacks for?"

"I suppose their supplies came packed inside them. So what's the big deal with that?"

"Well, when those burlap bags were emptied, the miners would cut each bag in strips and place the strips in the bottom of their sluice boxes. Those bags were used to catch the fine gold, the stuff we call gold dust. After a few days of mining, they would replace the strips of burlap with new ones, and pick out the flakes of gold stuck in the fabric of the burlap. Gold was so plentiful when they first started mining, a person could pick up gold nuggets right off the ground. It was impossible for the old miners to pick out all the gold from those bags. There's only one way to remove all that gold. DB, you've discovered a pile of gold dust just waiting to be mined."

"That's a great idea, Bob. But how do you mine a gunnysack pile?"

I watched a greedy smile spread across his face. His eyes glazed over. His body language made it clear. *I've got you now, DB.*

Bob leaned forward. "I know exactly how to mine that pile of gold, but I want fifty percent of the take. If you agree, I'll tell you how to do it."

"Here's what I'll do, Bob. I'll give you the location of the deserted mine site. Then you can mine the gold, and I'll take fifty percent of the take."

"I'm too busy to go to the west coast of Alaska and look for gunnysacks in the barrens somewhere. It sounds like a wild goose chase to me. No thanks, DB."

"You just made my point, Bob. You share your idea with me, and I'll give you ten percent of the gold recovered, if I'm lucky enough to recover any."

"It's a deal! Let's shake on it." Bob jumped out of his chair and extended his hand.

He's too eager, I thought. *I should have held out for a better split.*

"DB, you're not as smart as I thought. You should have figured this out for yourself. You burn the gunnysacks, collect all the fine ashes and dirt after the fire dies down, and bring it back home in pails. Then you can process the dirt during the winter months. It will be a slow process, but it beats watching the snow fall all winter."

"It's a great idea, Bob, but to tell you the truth, I'm not sure I can find that site again. It's been more than three years since I was there. I spent a lot of time wandering around the barrens with no landmarks. I made lots of turns with limited visibility before I stumbled on that old mining camp. There's only a slim chance that I can find it again."

About mid-summer of 1983, we had a helicopter stationed in Unalakleet, Alaska, doing land survey work. One morning, Eddie Gunter, our chief pilot, called the office to report that his helicopter radio was not working. He needed a replacement before he would venture out into the "vast nothing." Fearing he'd get lost in the Alaskan barrens, I agreed to bring him a replacement that very day and filled my Navajo Chieftain with fuel. This 'twin engine sports model' could get the radio to his location before lunch.

"Lovie, how would you like to take a little flight over to Unalakleet? We can take the replacement radio over and be back home before dark."

"Honey, you're so full of it! Don't you think I know that it won't be dark again for another month?"

"Okay. I'll have you home before midnight. Besides, this is a great opportunity for us to look for that old mine and the gunnysack pile of gold."

"Now you're talking! I'll pack a lunch and be right over. I've been thinking about that gold ever since you talked to Bob. You get the Navajo and radio ready." Carol's excited voice demonstrated her preoccupation with the "lure of gold."

"Lovie, you seem awfully eager. You're getting 'gold fever,' aren't you?"

"Greed for gold is a good thing. Hurry, let's get going."

About an hour later, I had both engines turning and copied my IFR clearance for departure. Cleared directly to Unalakleet, I climbed to 12,000 feet and squawked 5153; Talkeetna had a thin overcast. When

I felt the wheels retract, I flew into the clouds. With a thirty-degree bank to the left, we were on our way in search of gold. We had flown about twenty miles when we broke out of the overcast. Mt. McKinley hung off my right wing tip. At 12,000 feet, with no clouds to obstruct our view, the sight of the "Big One" filling the sky was spectacular!

Flying at 280 miles per hour, it didn't take long to reach the west coast of Alaska. With the coastline in sight, I cancelled my IFR clearance and proceeded on my own navigation. I had enough fuel to look for the old mining site for an hour or so before landing in Unalakleet to deliver the radio.

I flew at 3,000 feet and slowed the twin to 120 miles per hour. "I remember that mining camp was situated in a gully. All the cabins were nearly rotted away. Look for any horizontal lines in a creek bed."

We flew a large grid pattern for nearly an hour, finally gave up the search and headed for Unalakleet.

"All I saw were reindeer, Honey. Nothing looked like old buildings or a mining site to me."

"I'll get the radio changed out and fill the tanks. We still have time to search for another hour before we head home."

***

With the twist of a single screw, the old radio slipped from the rack that held it in place, and the replacement was quickly installed.

"Give this radio a try, Eddie."

"Unalakleet Radio, this is Helicopter 5100 Charlie. How do you copy me?"

"Helicopter 5100 Charlie, you are loud and clear."

"Okay, DB, I'm ready to go back to work. I'll round up the surveyors and get some work done today."

Carol and I discussed our flight plan for the search of the lost gunnysack mine. I decided to retrace my flight of four years earlier in hopes of locating that old village. With thin clouds overhead, I had to find the site today or it would probably be lost to me forever. I seldom flew to this area of Alaska, and would never make a special trip back this way looking for burlap sacks that might contain gold flakes.

Carol and I departed Unalakleet and flew north along the coastline. I saw many ravines that resembled the one I followed four years ago. I throttled the engines back, added ten degrees of flap, and slowed the twin to 100 miles per hour.

"Lovie, I'm going to turn up the next gully. If it turns left and then narrows, we may have the right drainage. Look for thick creek brush and anything horizontal."

In the natural world, most lines are vertical. Trees and brush grow skyward; mountains and hills reach upward. Man-made objects like houses, docks, roads and trails, however, appear horizontal. *If only I could get this Navajo to fly as slow as a helicopter. I can't see straight down. The wing is in the way!*

"Honey, Honey! What's that below us?" Carol pointed to an area filled with thick creek brush. It was easy to make out horizontal lines mixed among the foliage. I made a left turn over the area and spotted the pyramid-shaped pile of trash.

"It looks different with all the green leaves, but I think you've found it, Lovie. I owe you a cigar when we return home. Good work!"

I climbed while keeping the site in view. I got a radio fix from Unalakleet and Nome, and marked the site on my aviation sectional. *I'm getting smarter. This time I brought a map with me.* I snapped a couple of 35mm shots with my Nikon camera and set a course straight for Talkeetna.

Carol was excited about our find. "Dennis, let's come back next month and mine for gold. I feel the gold beckoning to me. You've got to trust a woman's intuition. I know it's there. We better do it before someone else finds it."

"Lovie, it could take weeks to burn that pile of rubbish. It might rain every day and not burn at all."

"Trust me on this one, Honey. I have a good feeling about this."

"Okay, okay! I'll make it happen next month. But you have to make me a deal. If we find one ounce of gold, you have to smoke a Cuban cigar with me at Simon & Seafort's Restaurant. No little wimpy puffs either. You gotta match me, puff for puff, right there in front of everybody." I figured that would scare her off, but no such luck.

"You've got a deal. Puff for puff, and I get half the take of your poke."

"Lovie, you drive a hard bargain. It's a deal!"

A month later, we arrived at the old mining site. I landed the helicopter and Carol set up a temporary camp. Carol loved "bush" life. We would soon feel at home in our 8 x 10 canvas tent.

I spent my first hours poking around the old site with a pitchfork, making sure there were no more bear traps hiding beneath the tundra. I determined the site to be safe as Carol lit the fire to prepare our first meal.

Carol's idea of a bush camp included rugs on the floor of the tent and folding lawn chairs next to a collapsible table. I settled into my lawn chair while Carol poured some "bush" coffee.

"It's good to be married to an Indian squaw," I told her. She called herself "Fire Starter," and once again had lived up to her name.

We had flown a Hughes 500 to our bush home and planned to remain there fourteen days. We had everything necessary to survive our adventure except food, but we could fly to Nome for groceries. We had reserved room onboard for the 50 five-gallon pails that we planned to fill with the fine material remaining after the gunnysacks were burned. Hopefully, the contents would render gold after processing.

Before day's end, we gathered rocks and built a fire ring about six feet in diameter. My "Fire Starter" soon had a large blaze ready for a "test run." When the flames leaped high into the sky, I used the pitchfork to toss the rotten gunnysacks into the inferno, but saved the old cans and some bottles.

"Maybe we'll get back here some day and pick up some of these antique bottles." But for the moment, the lure of gold held our attention.

The burlap bags were full of moisture, so each time I pitched one onto the fire, it would sizzle for a long while. Beating the blaze to a smolder, the moisture-laden bags eventually surrendered to the heat of the hot coals, then I would heap on another load of gunnysacks. By the time we turned in for the night, we were exhausted, but convinced we would be able to burn up the entire burlap pyramid

***

"Lovie, it's kind of you to let me sleep while you make breakfast. How can I thank you?"

"You could go over and get the fire stoked. There should be some hot coals that will take off if you stir them up a bit and throw on a few dry sticks."

"Can I have breakfast first? I'm starving."

"Okay, but we'd better keep that fire burning. This weather won't last forever."

When I planned this adventure, one of my main concerns was being able to find enough dry wood to keep the fire burning because no trees grew in the area. The creek bed, however, was full of dead brush. When the supply of tundra brush was depleted, I figured I could tear off boards from the collapsed buildings to feed the fire.

Carol always kept a tidy camp. After each meal she washed the dishes, cleaned up around the tent, and returned every item to its designated spot. When she finished her chores she assisted me with the burning process. Most afternoons, a light drizzle settled in and lasted into the night. But the hot fire kept us warm and dry. The rain seemed a nuisance at first, but merely added to our adventure as the days wore on. Nature provided the perfect romantic setting each night: cuddling in a dry tent, next to a warm lady, and listening to the raindrops tap against the tent roof.

By the end of the first week we had reduced the gunnysack pile considerably, and allowed the flames to die down. Using some creek brush branches, I swept away the top layer of ashes, figuring the gold flakes would settle to the bottom of the fire pit. With the aid of some strong winds and the sweeping action of the brush brooms, the ashes lifted and followed the gale across the barren land.

I was anxious to see if any gold flakes were visible in the pit, so I dug up a couple spades of heavy material, and spread it over an old sheet Carol had brought along for that purpose.

"Lovie, come look at this material. I don't see one gold flake among all this sand and gravel."

"I doubt you'd know a gold flake if you saw one. You're looking for something bright and shiny. When we leave next week, we take whatever we've found here, be it gold or gravel. Remember, it's not the gold that matters. It's the search for the gold that makes it worthwhile."

Before darkness returned I had the fire roaring again, and heaped on more decaying gunnysacks. Boards from the rotted cabins proved to be good fuel. As the pile diminished, I noticed the sacks became dryer. On the evening of the eleventh day I threw on the last of the burlap bags. I still had a large pile of dry wood stacked up, and threw on about half of it. Soon it blazed high into the night, sending thousands of sparks skyward. The job was finished. We looked at each other and gleefully danced about the fire pit, Indian style, celebrating our victory over the gunnysacks.

The following morning we slept in for the first time on this trip, stirring from our beds in late morning. We had no watches; the time of day was never of much importance in the bush. Only a few hot coals remained, so I grabbed the shovel and began to throw the ashes into the air. The breeze lifted the ash above our heads and it drifted away. When I finally reached the dirt bottom, the hole was more than a foot beneath the surface of the soft tundra. Evening came but the soil was still too hot to work. I used the shovel to move the hot material to the inside of the rock fire ring, banking it up to make it burn faster. In the morning, I planned to filter the dirt, and shovel the fine into pails.

I brought along a miner's screen, a brass bucket with a wire mesh bottom that fit perfectly over the 5-gallon pails. While I shoveled the dirt onto the screen, Carol shook the pail, causing the finer material to sift through. After several shovels full, the larger rocks and debris were discarded and the process repeated. I was surprised to see so many pieces of metal, glass, and bone fragments.

By the end of the second day we had screened all the material. I even scraped the bottom of the fire pit, and put it through the sieve.

"Well, Lovie, we have forty-seven pails of fine and I've yet to see one gold flake. Let's haul this dirt home, but I doubt that our efforts will make your flowers grow any better."

"Honey, I'll admit I was hoping to see something that looked like gold by now. Maybe now, we know why the old miners left this place. I'm still going to haul it all home. I'll think of some use for it. Besides, it represents the memory of a dream, all our hard work, and the foolhardy notion we had about gunnysack gold."

I didn't have a scale, but my best estimate weighed the pails in at more than eighty pounds each.

"I admire your grit, Lovie. We had a great time here even if we are going home gold-less. It will take four trips to Unalakleet to get this dirt to the airport. I'll have Eddie call the office. They can send the Navajo over to pick up the pails. I'll try to get it done today so we can head home tomorrow."

The next day our pilot arrived at Unalakleet with the twin. Carol stayed in camp to tidy up while Eddie Gunter and I waited at the airport.

"DB, I can't believe you had me call for the Navajo just to haul a ton of dirt home. When the office hears about this payload, they will laugh their butts off."

"This was Carol's idea. Tell them to laugh at Carol. Then we'll see who has the last laugh."

"Not funny, DB. You know we would never make fun of Carol. She could make life miserable for all of us."

"Well, since that issue is cleared up, I would suggest we keep this dirty little secret between the two of us. Tell the boys to unload the pails behind the hangar. If Carol even gets wind of a snicker from anyone at the office, you'll all be in deep trouble. Do you get my drift?"

"I get the point, DB. You'd better get that eggbeater back to your campsite. Tell Missy Carol 'Hi' from me."

The wheels disappeared into the belly of the aircraft as the twin made a pass over the airport. I returned to Carol and camp with a special surprise that Eddie had given me.

"Honey, what's that under your jacket? You know you can't hide anything from me."

"You build us a little fire and I'll show you what I brought you, Missy Fire Starter."

We sat together in our lawn chairs with our feet warming by the flames. I pulled out the bottle of wine and put it on our camp table.

"How nice of Eddie to think of us. This will help us celebrate our gold and warm our night." Carol was right. The wine warmed us up just right.

The next morning we packed the Hughes for the trip home. "Honey, I'm leaving the tent here, just as it stands."

"Why would you want to do that?"

"Well, I figure the old miners left their shelters when they deserted camp. If we find even one flake of gold in those pails, we may be the last miners to leave this place. I put a note in that wine bottle telling why we came here, and a little about our experiences mining for gunnysack gold. Someday, someone might come to this old mining camp just like we did. I want to leave our story behind."

"Buckle up, Lovie. It's time to go home." No one inquired about the forty-seven pails of dirt. They sat unmolested behind the hangar until Thanksgiving. During that holiday week Carol spent nearly five hundred dollars of her Christmas money to purchase a gold processing shaker table, and set it up in a heated room in the hangar. Bob Young came by to show her how to process the fines.

I was on my way to my office several days later when I heard Carol yelling across the hangar. "Honey, get over here. I've got something to show you."

"Yeah, Lovie. Looks exciting all right. What have you got there? It looks like a bunch of black sand to me. I had hoped that you and Bob could come up with something better than sand."

Carol handed me a large magnifying glass. "Look closely at that black sand with this, smarty pants."

Through the glass, I could clearly see the glitter of gold sprinkles. "Lovie, I think I see small dots of gold in with that black sand. Maybe this shaker table is going to do the job for you, after all."

"Honey, you have no idea what you're looking at. Those aren't just gold dots in black sand. All that black sand is fine gold. We've struck it rich!"

"Not so fast, Lovie. You've only processed a few pounds of material. You still have more than forty-six pails remaining. You have lots of work to do before you're rich."

Our electric shaker table had a grooved plastic sheet with small indentations cut horizontally. Water washes over this specially designed top as the table shakes. The lightweight dirt, sand, and trash are flushed away leaving the heavier material like gold trapped in the grooves. About one-half cup of material can be processed at a time, making the procedure very time consuming.

Someone has to watch constantly to insure maximum reward.

By the first of May, the process was completed. Bob helped us remove the tarnish from the gold. It sparkled as only gold can. It was time to divide the take. Bob had a set of gold screens he used to size the gold. Each size category was placed in a special bottle. The precious metal glistened as we placed the bottles in straight rows on my desk.

"Well, Bob, what's your take?"

"I weighed each bottle with Carol looking over my shoulder. I recorded the weight of each on a tag and glued it on the bottle. You've been very successful in this mining operation."

"Okay, Bob. Cut to the chase. What's your take?"

"I'm taking nine ounces and a few pennyweight. That leaves you two more than 80 ounces. That's a good return for a pile of gunnysacks!"

We were delighted with our success, maybe even gloating a bit. Carol boasted, "I plan to save my share, Honey. What do you plan to do with yours?"

"I've been thinking about investing in a new fruit computer. I think it's called an Apple."

"I should have figured you would buy some kind of toy. Sounds like a waste of money to me. They say those new computers are just a passing fancy. You'll be sorry."

***

Simon & Seafort's Restaurant sits on a bluff overlooking Cook Inlet. Carol and I sat at the large walnut bar, looking at our reflections in the massive mirror with an enticing array of spirits lined up in front. Also reflected in the mirror were the images of old Alaskan sourdoughs depicted in the paintings hung on the wall behind us, some of them miners who toiled in Alaska's gold fields decades earlier.

"Well, Lovie, you get the first puff of this Cuban."

"How did you manage to find a Cuban cigar in Alaska? Look at that thing. It's nine inches long. You surely don't expect to smoke it all tonight, right here in front of everyone?"

"I spent a lot of money on the black market getting this Cuban for you, Lovie. We're smoking every inch of it just like you promised. I'll light it up. You get the first puff."

Grandfather

The day after Thanksgiving we left Nebraska and started our 3,500-mile trek to Anchorage, Alaska. On my birthday, December 18, we arrived in the "Great Land," and were greeted by the cold reality of minus forty degrees. Carol and I were young and strong; we welcomed a new adventure. At first, Alaska appeared an inhospitable frozen waste, but later it proved to be the land of opportunity. I wanted answers to questions that troubled my young soul. In time, I discovered that experience changes the questions, and that there are no answers, only solutions.

We spent three years in the Canadian Arctic then moved on to Alaska, hoping that vast wilderness would fulfill our wildest dreams. We settled in Talkeetna,

Alaska, with our young sons, Cory and Les. The old log house on the village airstrip was the perfect home for a young bush pilot and his family; I parked my airplane in the driveway next to the Jeep.

It was a couple winters later when Grandfather came to live with us. At first, I considered him just another mouth to feed. We expected his visit to be short, but as summer came and went he settled in, and we quickly became attached to him. I recognized he wanted to stay as long as we'd have him, because we symbolized the only family he had.

The years melted away like icicles. The boys grew up and faced new challenges, and Grandfather enjoyed each one with them. When the boys went fishing, he was there. He wasn't much of a fisherman, but assisted them in landing the "big ones." If a bear approached, he helped chase it away. During the winter months he rode behind the boys on the back of the snow machine, hanging on with all his strength. He fell off a few times. It must have been painful, but he always got back on and never complained about the rough ride.

Carol often said, "Grandfather is precious to the boys. He cares for them in ways you and I can't. They share their secrets with him and trust him fully, sensing that Grandfather loves them unconditionally. He never reveals the mischief those boys get into."

His care for the boys helped Carol and I, now actively involved with the affairs of our business. Occasionally, we had to spend a night away from home and it was comforting to know Grandfather's careful eye watched when we were gone. Observing Grandfather grow older brought sweet sorrow. I recognized that old age would someday overtake him, but tried not to think about it.

Life in Alaska presented us with extraordinary experiences. We delighted in the good times, and struggled through the difficult ones. We took in David, our third son, and Grandfather accepted him right away. Before long the three boys and Grandfather were known as the "fearsome foursome."

David was the first to learn to fly, and Grandfather loved being in the air with him. Whenever there was an extra seat, he took it. If he wasn't allowed to ride along, he would wait patiently at the hangar for David's plane to return.

One day while driving back from Palmer, Alaska, Les, our youngest, said, "Look at that, Dad, a spotted moose." It was a Holstein cow that had strayed from a local dairy. That day I began to think about introducing the boys to a new environment.

"Carol, what would you think about moving to Mexico for a year to expose the kids to a different way of life? The boys have spent all their years in the North. It's time for them to get a new perspective." In spite of all I'd experienced and learned, I knew that Alaska wasn't the answer to everything.

Grandfather had lived with us for more than ten years when we decided to spend some time in Mexico with the boys. It was a wise choice. Alaska opened our eyes to new horizons, but a warm fantasy is more inviting than a cold winter day. The change would do us good.

Dave lived in his own cabin. It was agreed that Grandfather would stay behind with him in Alaska. Our hearts were heavy as we contemplated life without him, but Cory and Les realized that Grandfather would be happier with Dave. He could continue his daily walks around the village visiting people he knew, and greeting strangers. He was losing his hearing, but he didn't care what most people had to say anyway. He was satisfied to see them, and know all was well.

Christmas in Mexico promised to be lonely without family to help us celebrate. Then Dave and Grandfather surprised us with a visit. During this joyous reunion, we showed them the local sights, played on the beach, and fed them all the Mexican food they could hold. When it came time for Dave to return North, we hoped Grandfather would stay in Mexico, but he chose to go back to Alaska. The heat was too much for an old guy; he missed his home in the snow.

Dave married Julie and little Sophie was their first blessing. Despite Grandfather's advancing years, he helped care for her. He stayed by her side and protected her as she learned about her world. His hearing was nearly gone, but he had no trouble understanding Sophie's words. She talked to him constantly even though he couldn't hear, and had nothing to say. He gave her a special smile when she hugged him. If she didn't give him enough attention, Grandfather pushed against her until she responded with the hugs he loved.

The years sped by faster than the express train through Talkeetna. Cory joined the Army, and Les moved out on his own to attend college. Carol and I were forced to discover life without them. We were living in Colorado, where Carol attended the university, when I surprised her with an unexpected request.

"Lovie, let's go back home to Talkeetna. I need to see our friends and family again."

"Dennis! I've been begging to go back for a long time. I've lost track of all the countries we visited and lived in during the last few years. If you're done tramping around the world, I'm ready to go back."

We arrived in Talkeetna unannounced in September 1992. I felt like a stranger in the land that had been my home for many years. *Why had we stayed away so long?* Our one-year trip to Mexico turned into three years, visiting and living in a dozen countries in Central America, Asia, and Europe. We chased after adventure, and squandered Alaska.

No one greeted us when we arrived at the airport, but I was drenched with "welcome home" memories. Moisture hung in the morning air, dripping from the leaves and scrawny tree limbs. The mist touched our faces like angel kisses. Locals call this weather "dry rain." It felt good on my skin. I breathed in the sweet smell of wet vegetation decaying among the black crowberries. Gold and crimson leaves drifted slowly among the dark spruce trees.

"We're home, Lovie!"

We flew to Talkeetna intending to surprise Dave and his family; his home a short distance from the airport. Hand in hand we strolled in silence down the wet, gravel road. After only a couple blocks we saw a little girl and Grandfather coming our way. Sophie was only three, but was safe with Grandfather at her side. We stood quietly and watched them approach. They didn't notice us. Sophie jabbered and Grandfather listened, completely absorbed with the little girl's antics.

Sophie picked up a stone and shared her treasure. She tossed it into the air as her laughter filled the morning. Grandfather slowly retrieved the stone, and placed it in her hand. Sophie kicked at the leaves and Grandfather tried to catch them.

"Run faster. I'll race you. Let's go." The little girl's chatter made him pick up his pace. Grandfather struggled to keep up, but obviously was enjoying himself. They continued our direction and we waited for them to notice us. Finally, Sophie saw us standing on the road, stopped, and moved closer to Grandfather.

"I'm Sophie. Who are you?"

She had been born while we were away and did not know us, but Grandfather did. He was delighted to see us.

"Sophie, I'm Dennis and this is Carol. We've been gone a long time. Your daddy sent us pictures of you. Of course, we know Grandfather. It's nice he can still walk with you."

"We're on our way to the airport to see Daddy. Do you want to come with us?"

"We'd love to walk with you, Sophie."

"Grandfather, you're looking old and somewhat battered. You should have taken better care of your teeth."

Sophie pulled Grandfather up close as if to protect him. She emphatically stated. "This is my dog!"

"Yes, he is yours, Sophie, but once he was ours. He took care of your daddy, and now he takes care of you."

The four of us walked to the hangar. I tried to hide the tears flowing freely down my cheeks, and wiped them away with my damp sleeves. The questions that led me away from Alaska remained unanswered. But I was certain of one thing; It was good to be home!

Grandfather left us a year later. He lived 96 dog years, always in perpetual motion, attentively caring for his children. He freely gave his life to all of us. He created magic in the lives of our boys, and grandchildren. His passing was tragic. But losing him opened my eyes to a truth about my life. He taught me that living well, and loving freely is the answer to the most important questions.

Don Got My Goat

Many people flee to Alaska in an attempt to escape their past. Over the years I've met killers and other felons trying to hide from justice. One old timer, once a gangster with Al Capone's mob, remained a fugitive, hiding in the bush until the statute of limitations expired. He eventually returned to society, redeemed by the passing of time. Some people change their identity in an attempt to avoid IRS collections. Often criminals are relocated in Alaska under the witness protection program. Alaska is a perfect place to hide in plain sight from dangerous thugs.

One day while purchasing a six-pack of brew at a Muldoon liquor store, I bumped into a scraggy-bearded, wild-eyed hippy. We exchanged pleasant greetings, but when I turned to leave, he stepped in front of me, blocking my exit.

"That must be your pickup truck parked there. I'm Don, and I'm looking for construction work. I'm the fastest and the best there is. If you hire me, you can fire the rest of your crew. No kidding! I wouldn't lie to you. Come over to my camper and meet my 'old lady' and three brats. She'll tell you how good I am."

"Slow down, friend. You talk way too fast. I am a builder. I'm presently working on this mall, but I don't need any help right now. Besides, you look stoned to me, and I don't hire druggies."

"No, no. I don't do drugs. I'll work the rest of the day for free. If you aren't happy with my performance, I'll go away and look for work somewhere else. It'll be your loss." I found his self-marketing approach interesting.

Don turned toward his camper and yelled. "Jean, get out here. I want you to meet my new boss." The camper door opened and Jean stepped out. She was a good-looking lady, slightly overweight, wearing tight blue jeans soiled with Alcan mud. Her hand-knitted sweater and the "no-bra" look revealed a more than ample chest. Three little ragamuffins straggled out of the camper and lined up behind her.

She pointed at her husband. "There's no better worker in California than Don. We need the money. Give him a chance. You won't be sorry."

"Jean, how long have you folks been in Alaska?"

"We've been here about thirty minutes. Except for fuel stops, we haven't stopped since the Beaver Crossing Border Station."

"Well, Don, you're right about one thing. You do things fast. Do you know anything about electrical work?"

" I'm the best electrician you'll ever find."

"Ok, ok. Stop with the hard sell. Go help those two electricians install some underground pipe. If you last the day, I'll pay you. If you can't cut it, disappear before I return."

When I arrived back on the job site around quitting time, everyone had gone home except Don, sitting on the front bumper of his truck, drinking a beer. I walked over and extended my hand. "I see you're still here. How'd your first day go?"

"I'm still here, aren't I? You'll have to plan a lot more work each day to keep me busy. We finished that project before quitting time. I need to have lots of work laid out so I don't get bored."

"You finished laying all that pipe? I figured it would take two days, at least."

"For those slugs on your crew, you're probably right. I'm the California 'Road Runner.' That job is done, with no thanks to those two deadbeats."

I checked Don's work. The job was finished, the quality was good, and he was fast. *How could I be so lucky*? "Don, where are you spending the night?"

"I planned to stay right here in this parking lot in my camper. Is that a problem?"

"That might work until about 2 a.m. and then you'll be arrested. You're in Anchorage, Alaska. We may look uncivilized, but we have cops here. I live a few miles from town. Follow me home, and you can park your camper in my yard for a couple of nights."

"Thanks, Dennis, we'll do that. Hey, do you want one of these beers? When I found out you own the liquor store here, I had the gal put a couple of six-packs on your tab. I didn't think you'd mind buying me a beer. You don't, do you? After all, I'm worth a beer or two."

"Is everyone from California as gutsy as you?"

"No, just me."

Don and his family set up two tents in my yard, backed their camper up between them, and unloaded lots of stuff. "I think they're gypsies." Carol whispered. "I hope we're safe with them living in the yard."

I was about to disagree about them being gypsies when Don proceeded to build a campfire in the front yard. "I'm not sure what we have here, Lovie, but there goes the grass."

Everything Don said proved to be true. Before long, he and one other worker had replaced the five "slugs," as Don called them. Carol was right about the gypsy behavior, too, but we learned that Don and his family could be trusted.

Carol and Jean shared a free spirit and became good friends. From the beginning they collaborated on evening meals, which we often consumed outside on picnic tables. One evening several weeks later - after a few bottles of wine - Don opened up and told me about his life in California.

"I'm a big game hunter. It's an addiction I can't overcome. I started hunting years ago in California. I ignored the hunting regulations, thought they were for sportsmen, not real hunters. My best friend Leroy often hunted with me. He was never concerned about hunting out of season. Together, with five other hunters, we took several bears from Shasta-Trinity National Forest in one year. We hunted trophy elk, deer, and a few desert sheep."

He continued his story leaning back and stretching his long legs. "The night I left California, Leroy called to warn me that I was about to be arrested for poaching. I was shocked because Leroy was the County Sheriff. I guess one of our six hunting partners was an informant for Fish and Game. Leroy wasn't certain who the informant was, but he had no choice but turn over all the evidence to save himself from being prosecuted. I guess I should be grateful that he warned me, and allowed me time to escape."

"So much for loyal friends! What did you do next?"

"I threw everything I could into the camper and left for Alaska that night."

"So what's your plan now, Don?"

"Well, the statute of limitations is seven years, so I'm considering returning when it runs out."

"You really plan to go back?"

"Someday we will. For the time being, we're starting over here in Alaska. I've put all that crime stuff behind me. Jean and I are Mormons now."

"Don, what do you mean by crime stuff? Is there more than poaching?"

Don didn't answer right away. He put his wine glass down, and took several big hits from the bottle. "Well…I was a cat burglar for years, probably ten or more. I was charged several times, but never convicted."

"Let me get this straight. You stole cats? Is there money in that?"

"Dennis, you've been north way too long. Cat burglars, you know, they scale tall buildings, somewhat like mountain climbing, sneak in an open window, and fill two or three pillowcases with anything of value. Usually, I'd fill a suitcase with jewelry, cameras, and coin collections, then take the elevator down to the lobby, and simply walk out. A security guard never stops a person from leaving a building. Now, with all the new security cameras, it's much harder to make a living as a 'cat burglar.' Anyway, I've retired from that life."

"Hey, man, is there anything else I should know about you?" I asked pointedly.

He put down the wine bottle and poked at the fire. I waited quietly, secretly hoping there was no more.

It was late; I started to push myself out of my chair when Don broke the silence. "Well…this is difficult." He paused, looking straight ahead. I leaned in to hear him better.

"Don, are you going to finish this, or leave me hanging all night?"

"I'm in big trouble, Dennis. I'm hiding from the mob. I transported drugs for a key player for a few years, nothing real big, just a few kilos from one place to another. I would exchange the merchandise for money, and then take the cash to my 'man.' My take was five percent, and I was never short except for the night I fled California. Earlier that night I had made a delivery. When Leroy called with the warning, I kept the money and took off. It was a big mistake, but there's nothing I can do about it now."

"How much money are you talking about?" I was both curious and cautious.

"I have $96,000 hidden in the spare tire under my pickup. I can't send it back. If I do, my 'man' will tell the Fish and Game where I'm hiding, just to get even. No one in California knows we're here, but I know they have people looking for me. Do you have any idea what they will do if they find me?"

"I don't want to know. We never had this conversation, Don. If you promise me you won't get into any trouble here in Alaska, I'll keep your secret. I can't afford to lose you."

I wondered if Don had shared the truth about his life. It was an incredible story. I became convinced that he had been straight with me, and was serious about his new faith as a Mormon.

Since I owned an old Piper Super Cub, when Don expressed an interest in learning to fly, I gave him lessons. We planned a mountain goat hunt in late August so one afternoon, we knocked off work early and flew from the Birchwood Airport to our intended hunting area. I let Don fly from the front seat as I gave him flight instruction from the back. He had several hours of instruction, and was making good progress toward becoming a pilot. We followed the Glenn Highway to the Knik River, then turned right and followed the Knik east, to Hunter Creek. Don climbed with the terrain as it rose toward Hunter Creek Glacier. We flew above the glacier where the ice meets the mountain, with the rocks a few hundred feet off our right wing tip. I was watching for big game below when I suddenly caught a view of the mountain in front of us.

"Don, we're below the ridge! Full power, climb, climb, climb!"

Don had flown into a blind canyon. We couldn't turn around without hitting a mountain wall. I looked past his left shoulder and saw the airspeed indicator at 40 m.p.h. The ridge was approaching and I yelled, "Don, I've got it, we're going to crash!"

I pulled back on the stick and we inched up a few more feet. The plane could no longer climb. It hung on, propeller shuddering. The boulders slid under us with a couple inches to spare. The plane quit flying; the nose fell. I instinctively pushed the stick forward. The mountain descended abruptly, saving us from crashing. I regained control of the plane over a drainage appropriately named Troublesome Creek.

"You just about killed us, you idiot! What were you doing? We came within inches of dying."

"Oh, quit your whining. We made it, didn't we? Learn to live on the edge. That was the best rush I've had in years. Stop and think about it. Wasn't that great?"

"That was too close for me, Don. I don't want you to ever take such a big chance again, not with me onboard, anyway."

I was ready to go home, but Don had a way of making things seem acceptable, and convinced me to continue our search for mountain goats. We flew toward the area where the Knik Glacier pushes up against Mount Palmer to form Lake George. Rushing water cuts away at the glacier where it meets the mountain, in an area called "the Gorge." We followed Troublesome Creek, and turned right, flying along the shoreline. Out of danger, I felt safe flying from the back seat, and assigned Don the job of aerial scouting. We spotted some moose and a couple of bears in the valleys, and mountain goats on every mountainside. We flew around the lake and made the decision to hunt on the north side.

Lake George fills with water each spring from the snowmelt. When the water level rises high enough, it erodes the Knik Glacier. The lake, known as the "Toilet Bowl" by the locals, spills most of its contents leaving a small body of water called Inner Lake George. It wasn't legal to land with wheels on the lakeshore, so we would have to persuade a friend with a floatplane to bring us back to this prime hunting location.

***

Eager to get some bush flying time, Jim Baker agreed to fly Don and me to Lake George. He had been one of my student pilots, and just received his floatplane rating. This was his first flight since buying a Super Cub on floats, and I was his first paying passenger.

The fruity, and pungent scent of the high bush cranberries lingered along the shoreline of Fire Lake as the morning fog gave way to the sun's rays, streaming over the mountain's rim. The trail leading to the floatplane was slippery with morning dew. I slid to a stop at the lake's edge leaving half my load on the shore for the next relay to the plane's cargo compartment. Stepping onto the float with the loaded pack and gear, I edged toward the cargo door near the aft of the plane. Edo floats are narrow on top and more slippery than grass, so I reached for the wing strut to steady myself. But with one misstep I landed on the lake bottom with water up to my knees.

"Okay, so my feet are wet already. No big deal! Help me with this gear, will you, Jim? I don't want to drop this load in the water."

"Here's the problem, Dennis. Look at this frost on the floats. You're lucky you didn't fall in ass first. Stand still and hand me the gear. I'll stow it for you."

I waded back to shore and sat on the bumper of my pickup. Taking off my boots, I dumped out the water, and then squeezed most of the moisture from my wool socks. Stuffing my feet back into soggy socks and boots was a struggle.

"Dennis, don't you want to change into dry clothes?"

"Nah, Jim. I've been wet and cold before. I'll dry out after I set up camp. I can't wait to get out there. Let's go flying."

There wasn't much water left in Lake George when we arrived, just a narrow strip about a half-mile long and a few hundred feet wide. The water was black with glacier silt, making it impossible to spot the sand bars below the surface.

"Be careful, Jim. Land in the center of the body of water and slow the plane as quickly as you can. Taxi slowly to shore. Be wary of sandbars and shallow areas that we can't see."

Jim made a perfect landing and taxied slowly toward shore. About two hundred feet from the bank, the floats skidded against the sandy bottom and ground to a stop. "Now you see why I didn't bother to put on dry clothes. I'll have to wade to shore. Set my gear on the float, Jim." I stepped into twelve inches of freezing cold water.

"I hope you don't think I'm going to get wet, Dennis. I'll stay up here where it's dry, if you don't mind."

It took four trips to get all my gear to shore. I was soaked to my waist, and would need to build a fire as soon as Jim departed.

"Okay, Jim, I'll push you back and help you turn the plane around. With no wind you can take off from here. Keep the plane in the area where we landed and you'll be okay."

Jim lifted off, made a steep turn, flew over the camp, and disappeared north at the Knik Glacier. Stillness filled the gorge. Within a few minutes, I built a large fire, mounted my boots on two sticks nearby to dry, and then draped my jeans over the boots. Wearing only my briefs I began setting up my tent.

Since Don had not arrived at the lake before my departure, he might not make it before dark. It was late afternoon when I heard the drone of a propeller and saw the floatplane heading toward me. Jim flew low overhead at about a hundred feet, wagged his wings on sighting my camp, and then made a shallow left turn to line up for another approach. His floats sliced through the water for another great landing. *Perfect, Jim, just the way I taught you.* The floats settled into the water, and he added power for a high-speed taxi to shore.

Waving my hands frantically above my head, I yelled, "No, no. Slow down. Slow down," but he ignored my warning. Perhaps he didn't see me.

At about the location where he struck the sand bottom on his previous landing, he chopped power. The plane skidded a few feet on the sand as the tail slowly rose above the lake. It continued to rise until the nose of the floats balanced on the sand, the plane vertical. It hovered a moment as if trying to decide whether to fall on its back or settle on the floats. The wind made the decision, and the plane resumed its correct position.

"That was close! What were you thinking of, you moron? I told you to land and taxi in slowly until you rubbed the bottom."

Don popped the door open and jumped out into ankle-deep water. "Man, that was a rush. Did you see that? We could have gone over. What a great start to a 'bitchin' hunt." Jim crawled out and stepped into the water. He looked sheepish.

"You came close to disaster, Jim."

"I know. Guess I let Don talk me into that high-speed taxi. He's never flown in a floatplane before, and has the ability to persuade a person to do utterly stupid stuff."

"Well, it's nice that you're sitting high and dry, but before you get too excited, remember that we have to get this plane back into water where it can float. That appears to be about 200 feet behind you."

We removed our gear from the Super Cub and stored it near the tent. Using a float pump, Jim pumped out the water that had accumulated, and we drained the fuel into four 5-gallon containers we had brought along. Finally, we removed all the light stuff, like seat cushions, survival gear, and even maps. Rocking the plane caused the floats to create a small wake under them. When the waves grew to a few inches, we attempted to move the plane. The right water rudder stuck in the sand, which allowed us to push the plane around that point until it faced the deeper water.

Jim wasn't "bush tough" and shivered in the cold water. "Guys, I'm whipped, not to mention wet and cold. Let's go to the tent, build up the fire, and warm ourselves with some hot tea. I could use something to eat." He started toward shore.

Don continued his efforts. "I think we can last a bit longer. Let's give her a few more pushes." He was talking to himself.

I followed Jim toward the tent. The lake water had been glacier only days ago, and I was freezing. Jim and I threw more wood on the fire and watched Don struggle alone until he finally stomped his way toward us, muttering under his breath.

"I can't believe my luck! I picked a couple of old ladies to hunt with." But in camp, Don moved in close to our fire. After several cups of tea, and more sticks of wood, I developed a plan.

"Jim, after you start the engine, Don and I will rock the floats from heel to toe. When she's rocking good, you give it full power. If we're lucky, we'll be able to get the plane to move forward an inch or two with each rocking motion."

The idea worked just as planned. Don and I struggled at the back of the floats with the propeller blast and water showering us. In about half an hour we had successfully moved the plane into deeper water where it could float. But we were frozen. It was painful walking in the knee-deep water. Jim yelled from the cockpit, "Go warm up and then bring me some fuel. I'm not getting out of this cockpit. I'll wait right here until you two bring enough gas to get me home."

Don and I threw more sticks on the fire and dug in our packs for dry shirts. We were too cold to dash back, so we backed up to the fire, rubbing our bodies to bring back feeling to our legs.

"We should make Jim wait out there," Don suggested. "Maybe he'll get discouraged and come back for the fuel. It's his plane. Why should we have to wade out there again for him?"

"Great idea, Don. If Jim has to wade ashore to retrieve his own fuel, and then haul those 5-gallon pails back to the plane, I doubt he'll remember to come and pick us up when our hunt's over. He'll remember how you talked him into that stupid high speed taxi, and how you refused to help him refuel his plane."

Don looked past me toward the plane. "I'm warmer now. Let's get this fuel out to Jim so he can get out of here before dark."

The fuel filled two old Gerry cans, plus two 5-gallon plastic pails. To avoid spilling the gas or contaminating it with water, we carried only one container each trip, and poured the contents back into the wing tanks, careful not to waste a drop. With the added weight, the floats soon settled back into the sand.

"Get it started, Jim. Don and I will try the rocking again. When she starts to move give her full throttle. Once you start moving, she'll fly."

Don yelled at Jim, "Don't forget to pick us up on Sunday afternoon."

"I don't think he can hear you, Don. Don't worry. If he doesn't return for us in a week or so, Carol will send someone else to find us. Besides, when Jean runs out of money she'll remember that you're out here in the bush waiting for a ride back to town."

"You're about as humorous as these wet clothes, Dennis."

Jim's plane lifted off with no problems. After his departure, I collected driftwood and fed the fire, sending a shower of sparks skyward. We spread our wet clothes on sticks around the blaze, but nothing would remove the cold from the core of my body. My insides still shook though I quit shivering some time ago. I couldn't have pissed even if I wanted to. This is a common problem for a guy when the cold grabs you, but, thank God, it's not permanent!

Don crawled into his down bag, lit his Coleman, and proceeded to read a paperback novel. Every few minutes, he broke into laughter, jabbering about something which made no sense to me whatsoever, and then returned to his reading.

"You don't seem to be suffering, Don. I'm frozen clean to the bone."

"You're just a wimp. You've got to get your mind off the cold. Think about something warm and fuzzy." He tore off the corner of the page he was reading, popped the paper into his mouth, and began to chew. Soon he broke into laughter again.

"Don, how can you laugh at a time like this? Are you stoned?"

"Of course, not. Have you forgotten that I'm a Mormon now?"

Frost invaded our camp sometime during the night. Its white signature coated everything when I crawled through the tent flap on all fours. My wet clothes were nearly dry on the side facing the fire; the backside was frozen stiff. I was blessed to have dry underwear and socks.

I built up the fire and warmed my butt before dealing with the shock of pulling on frozen jeans and shirt. After a few jumps and yelps, I came to tolerate the stiff pants. My frozen shirt became pliable when I held it over the fire on a stick. When I wrapped it around my cold body, it felt as comfortable as a warm quilt.

"Don, are we going hunting today, or are you going to sleep the morning away?"

"Since you're already up, why don't you be a good guy and fix some coffee? You could slice up some Spam and fry it. Yell at me when it's ready and I'll get up. I didn't sleep too well last night. I need a few more minutes."

"If you're going hunting with me, get your hairy butt out here and give me a hand, or I'm leaving without you."

Don crawled out through the tent flap sputtering about "givin' a guy a break." He whimpered while dressing, making me wonder if he'd ever faced a frosty morning before.

I deliberately neglected a watch when in the bush, but knew it was early morning. The sun's rays cut through the ragged mountaintops, but had yet to warm our camp. By the time we downed our first cup of coffee, the sun chased away the white frost. We were ready to hunt.

Don set up a spotting scope, and scanned the mountains to the north. "There're goats all over those hills. This should be a cakewalk. We'll bag a trophy."

"If I were you, Don, I'd take a good look. Those mountains are straight up and down, and there's a river between us and the game."

Don ignored everything I said. "Let's leave the tents set up here, and pack for one overnight. We should be able to get up that mountain, shoot our goat, and be back by tomorrow mid day."

I began to prepare for the hunt. "Hey, Don, dig out several of those heavy duty trash bags to protect our gear when we cross the river."

The river flowed from the lake at the beginning of the gorge. From the air it looked like a small creek, but standing at the river's edge revealed a raging torrent that deserved our respect. Water that had been frozen glacier the day before was now muddy with silt. The powdered rock and fine dirt turned the flow the color of hot chocolate – minus the hot!

Thankful we carried two 200-foot mountaineering ropes with our gear, I turned to instruct my hunting partner. "Don, lay the two ropes out on the bank and I'll tie them together in the middle." I tied a 'figure eight' to lace the ropes together.

"I don't think we need ropes for crossing this creek, Dennis. You're making a big deal out of a little water. It can't be more than a couple of feet deep."

"You might be right about the depth, but take a look at the force of those two feet. One missed step and you're going downstream. The bank gets steep below us. You won't get out until the end of the gorge. Of course, it won't matter, because you'll be dead from hypothermia before you reach the bottom."

"Come to think of it, the ropes might be a good idea when you consider the speed of the river. Do you want to go first, or should I?"

"I've done this before, Don. Listen and do as I say. Don't try to be creative, okay?" I removed my clothes and put them in the trash bag. With a long stick, I probed the river's bottom. With the rope tied around my waist, I stepped into the rushing water.

"Don, feed me the rope as I wade across to the other side. Keep it slightly tight but don't prevent me from moving. If I start to wash downstream, pull me back to shore. Another thing, try not to talk unless you have something important to say. I should be across in a few minutes. Can you make it that long without jabbering?"

The freezing water attacked my body. It felt like the scalding of boiling water. I gasped for breath as my muscles tightened from the intense pain. In the middle of the river, the water rose above my knees. I felt a strange numbness in my legs and struggled to think clearly. *Breathe in, breathe out. Keep moving. Just a little farther and you'll be on dry ground.* The stick helped to steady myself, while predicting the water's depth in the path ahead. If Don spoke, I heard nothing.

I arrived at the opposite bank and could hear Don yelling above the water's roar. "You made it, Dennis. Nothing to it! Don't sit there like an idiot. Put your clothes on." My mind told my body to move, but there was no response. After a few minutes, I pulled on my jeans and socks. The warmth of life came back helping me forget my time in the liquid ice pack.

"Okay, Don. Tie the rope to that tree stump and get naked. Strap everything to your pack and then come across, hand-over-hand, using the rope line. Don't let go, no matter what! We don't want your body to wash up near Anchorage."

Don took a couple of steps into the freezing water and quickly retreated, yipping. "It's too cold. I'm not going in there." He rubbed his legs to get the blood flowing again.

"If I can do it, you can do it. Remember, think about something warm and fuzzy."

"Great idea! I should have thought of that." He unzipped the top of his pack and removed his paperback novel. He fingered through a few pages, tore off a corner, and popped the piece of paper in his mouth.

"Don, are you hunting or reading a novel?"

"I'm not reading. I just need something to chew on. I'm coming."

"Next time, bring gum. I can't figure you out. Nobody chews corners from books. Get in the water. No more excuses. Move, now!"

Don fiddled with his gear for another ten to fifteen minutes before approaching the cold water again. He giggled as he stepped in and by mid-stream was laughing like a fool. I wondered if the cold had affected his mind. He had nearly reached the other side when the current washed his feet out from under him. He hung onto the rope with one hand. "I can't make it, Dennis. Do something. I'm going to drown with all this gear on my back."

"Quit being stupid. The water is only a foot and a half deep. Stand up."

Don regained his composure and stood up. He seemed surprised. "I guess you're right." The water did not reach his knees. In a few more steps he stood on the sandy shore, looked at me, giggled, and then pulled on his clothes.

"You know, Don, sometimes I think you're as tough as nails. But now, I'm beginning to think you're a little crazy. Which is it?"

"Whatever it takes to escape boredom." His eyes were glazed and a strange grin revealed his white teeth. "I'm ready to kill something. Look, Dennis, that looks like a Dall sheep on those rocks. It's only a 1000 yard shot. I could easily bring him down from here."

"You don't have a license to kill sheep. Sheep season is over."

"So what! I'm here to bring back a trophy. What an animal! He's carrying more than a full curl." Don rested his rifle on his pack and took steady aim.

He was about to squeeze the trigger when I kicked him in the ass. "You're an idiot. If Fish and Game catches you with that trophy out of season, you'll go to jail. Have you forgotten about California? You'll be looking at years behind bars."

"Don't worry about it. They won't catch me way out here. I gotta take the shot."

"You pull that trigger and I'm heading back to camp without you. The ropes come with me. You can stay on this side of the river until Jim returns. I'm not hunting with an idiot."

"Don't be so touchy. It's not your ass on the line."

"I won't be part of any poaching. I thought you put that life behind you."

"You're right. I'm a Mormon now. Old things have passed away. I was just kidding around with you."

"You could have fooled me." I was sure Don would have taken the shot if I hadn't been there to stop him. I understood what it meant to be addicted. A twinge of fear shot through my heart. *Can I trust him? What might he do to get a trophy?*

The "old timers" say that the word "alders" cannot be spoken as a single word. It must be preceded by a four or five letter expletive. Alders, smooth-leaved trees or shrubs of the birch family, grow out of the ground in clumps following the terrain. They turn and grow upward, so close to each other they appear to be holding hands. Traversing through an alder patch changes your language and your attitude.

We hiked a couple of hours in and out of alder patches, consistently working our way up the mountain until we were above tree line, far from the cursed alders and the bugs. The terrain abruptly changed to a steep incline. Fortunately, we found a mountain goat trail that helped us ascend without too much difficulty. The trail continued to narrow as the mountainside became more vertical. *Mountain goats may be at home here, but if we slip off this ledge, we'll fall straight to the bottom.*

"Dennis, look over there. That's a bunch of goats. Check 'em out. They all have trophy horns."

"Slow down, Don. They're a half-mile away and they don't know we're here yet, so take it easy. What are you doing? You can't pass me on this ledge." We were both carrying heavy packs with rifles tied to them, but Don insisted on passing. I flattened myself against the sheer mountain wall with the tips of my boots hanging onto the game trail. Don pushed his way around me, knocking the rocks loose under my left foot. I slid off the ledge, skidding to a stop on a shale pile, a hundred feet from the edge of the abyss. Shale is a flat piece of rock that breaks from the mountainside and slides down the slope, collecting in a loose pile.

"Don, come help me get me out of here. I can't move!" I was frantic.

"Be quiet. You'll scare the goats. Don't move or the shale will start sliding and you'll go over the edge. I'm going to shoot my goat and then I'll be back to get you off that shale pile. It's not my fault you fell down there." He disappeared around a rock without looking back.

The ledge on which I had been standing only moments earlier was just inches from my grasp. If I could reach the game trail, I could probably pull myself back onto firm ground.

"Don, get back here. I'm going to fall over." No response, not a sound. He was nowhere in sight. I wondered if he, too, had fallen off the trail. Perhaps his body lay splattered on the rocks below.

I pressed my face against the shale while my legs and arms spread out like a spider on a wall. I was not injured, but the fate of my life hung on the shale pile, eternity lay only 100 feet away. I reached forward with one hand; the entire hillside slowly slid down six inches. The game trail was forever out of my reach. If I could get my pack off, perhaps I could slow my downhill slide, but the release straps were against my chest. I rolled on my right side a little and reached for the buckle. This action caused me to slide five more feet toward my death. *Quit breathing. Think. Don't move. Think. God, I'm still moving downhill. Downhill leads to death.*

To my left, the shale was visible for as far as I could see. Fifty feet to my right, I spied terrain that would support me. It wasn't as vertical and displayed rocks, roots and shrubs. I would survive if I could work myself over there.

Stark terror eventually gave way to determination. I pushed myself, moving to the right and down. Simple math calculations showed I could reach firm soil near the edge of the precipice.

With each breath, I inched downhill, eventually arriving at the edge. A small root, probably years old, grew sturdy and steadfast to the right of my feet. Pieces of shale slid past me and smashed onto the valley floor.

I cautiously inched toward the precipice edge and pressed my foot against a rock that could sustain my weight. Now that my descent was temporarily halted,

I had time to rest and replenish my strength. I was feeling confident, until I saw the sow and her cub.

Below me, a brown bear sat with her offspring. I had no idea how long they had been watching my descent, patiently waiting for a meal to fall from the sky. Perhaps they had observed dinner fall from this ledge before. Every few minutes, the sow stood, grunted loudly, and clawed at the sky, as if reaching toward me. Thank God, her efforts were futile, as I hung far above her. Occasionally, a rock slid past me, and I watched as it fell over the edge. But the exploding rocks did not disturb the bear's vigil. The cub squealed and ran when the rocks plummeted downward, but soon returned to its mother for reassurance.

After an hour or so my strength and courage were renewed. I needed only two more feet to the right and I would escape this sliding slope. Of course, two feet down provided release also, but I preferred the option to the right. I pushed my foot against the rock and stretched as far right as I could. Then my foot slipped. My right knee brushed against a small root as I slowly slid downhill. I leaned further and grasped the root with my teeth when I could reach it. *I guess this is it. Well, bear, here I come. Finish me fast.*

Jaw muscles tire quickly; in a short time, my entire mouth racked with pain. I kicked wildly with my legs until I discovered a solid rock that held my weight - none too soon! Steadied on the rock, I grabbed another root with my right hand and jerked. It appeared sturdy, so I pulled myself up an inch or two until I could grasp a puny shrub. This strategy finally brought me to firm soil.

The mountain wasn't any less steep, but at least it wasn't moving downhill. I crawled to a well-secured rock and rolled over to a sitting position. It was the first time I sat upright since my ordeal had begun. The second thing I did was to unzip my fly and relieve myself next to the rock. I'd held it all afternoon. When one is near death's door, body functions lose their importance.

The sow paced back and forth below me, perhaps realizing her tasty meal had escaped. I was near collapse; my reserves now exhausted. Extreme fatigue overcame me, so I lay down behind the rock, too tired to remove my sleeping bag from my pack. Instead, I covered myself with a space blanket and passed out, welcoming a deep sleep.

The sun shone bright on the mountainside with the rays warming my silver space blanket. The warmth comforted my cold body. For a moment, I forgot I was clinging to the edge of a mountain. I scanned the valley for the sow, but she was gone. *Dear Lord, I'm so glad I didn't have dinner with the bears last night.*

I drank all the water from my canteen, and ate my dehydrated rations dry. They were pasty and tasted like sawdust, but I was famished. I thought about Don and concluded he must have fallen off the ledge. Otherwise, he would have returned for me. I feared to think of his fate; the sow and her cub might be feasting on his remains as I basked in the sunshine. I picked out some distinguishing landmarks near the place I had last seen the bear. I was the lucky one. *If I get off this mountain, and make it down to the valley, I'll come back to look for you, Don.*

I made my way downhill with ease, taking a direct path straight down when I could. Within a couple of hours, I was on the valley floor, looking up at the ledge where I had nearly lost my life. I found the rock where the bears had waited, then marked that spot by tying my space blanket - silver side up - to a rock and some bushes with nylon cord. If Don had fallen, this would be a good place to start a search. The silver blanket's reflection would be easy to see from the sky. I walked about a mile along the base of the cliff, expecting to find Don's body. There was plenty of bear scat, but no evidence of a fallen hunter.

After several hours, I gave up and started back to camp, crossing the river hand-over-hand when a Super Cub flew overhead. It made several passes over our tent, and then touched down on the sandbar near the river's edge just as I arrived. This pilot had exceptional skill, weaving among the driftwood piles. I would never have attempted to land a Super Cub in such terrain. The door popped open and someone crawled out of the back seat.

"Boy, am I glad to see you. I have a friend who may have fallen off the mountain. I marked the area with a space blanket near a rock where I believe he fell. I looked around, but couldn't find his body."

"Interesting. Can I see your hunting license?"

"Here's my license, but what about my friend? He could be injured and need help."

"Do you know it's illegal to land and hunt here on Lake George?"

"The regulations say it's illegal to land on the shore and hunt. I landed by floatplane and walked to shore. Forget hunting for a minute. My friend could be dead. What are you going to do about that?"

"I bet you think I really believe that story. I'm citing you for hunting illegally. See you in court." He handed me the ticket, and I tucked it in my billfold. I would deal with this problem later.

The agent's departure was as spectacular as his arrival, the plane again weaving between the driftwood piles before lifting off. *I wish I could fly like that. Well, maybe someday.* He paralleled the cliff line until he was out of sight. The sun was gone and so was the Fish and Game.

I built a fire in the dark and heated some water to prepare my camp food. It felt good to have a warm sleeping bag and a tent to protect me from the cold, but rest wouldn't come easy. My mind heard Don calling for help. I was certain he was gone. In two days, Jim would be back to pick me up. How could I tell Don's wife and three kids that he was dead? I prayed that someone would believe me. Surely his body would be found if only a proper search was conducted. I slept some, but did not rest at all.

The sun was high in the sky when the Super Cub that had visited me the night before returned to land on the beach. Again, the Fish and Game officer, Claude Aulmann, crawled from the plane and walked briskly in my direction. No 'howdy' or 'good morning,' he just scowled at me. "Let me see the ticket I gave you last night."

I pulled it from my billfold and handed it to him. He looked at it, tore it up and stuffed it in his pocket. "I checked the regs and you were right. You can land a floatplane here and hunt."

I was surprised to hear him admit his mistake. "That's great. Thank you. Now, how about my friend?"

"Well, maybe you are telling the truth about that, too. I'll fly around a bit and take a look. You better not be lying. I can still find something to charge you with, like a false report, for starters."

"You'll see a silver space blanket tied to a rock below the precipice. His body might be in that area. He's been missing for two days. He's probably dead by now."

The game warden left without a "good-bye." His plane disappeared, and the engine sound faded to nothing. It was late afternoon when the Super Cub landed the third time. I loathed hearing the report the officer was about to bring. The door of the plane opened, but the officer remained inside. I walked over to receive the bad news.

"Your friend is alive and walking this way. He's several miles away, but should be here by nightfall. I ticketed him for hunting without a license. I got one of you for a violation. I always find something."

"Thanks for finding my friend. I thought he was dead. Could I give you the phone number of our pilot, so you can call him and tell him we're ready for pick up?"

"When was he scheduled to pick you up? I'm sure he'll be back as arranged. I don't deliver messages. You guys have fun out here. I'll catch you when I can. You can count on it." He taxied through the driftwood and then disappeared over the Knik Glacier for the last time.

At least Don is alive. Alive! If he's alive, that means he left me on that shale pile to die. My attitude turned sour.

The valley was filled with the mist of dusk when I saw Don walking on the shoreline where it meets the mountain's rise. He probably spotted my campfire smoke long before I saw him. He used the rope tied at the river crossing, struggling hand-over-hand to traverse the raging waters, and arrived in camp, with clothes dripping, and his body shivering. His pack was heavy with goat horns strapped on top. With clenched jaws, I attempted to control my rage. Don had left me on that precipice to perish. I said nothing, waiting for him to explain his actions.

"I can see that you're angry with me, DB. Get over it. Both of us made it back safe. I had a great hunt. I saw more game than most hunters see in a lifetime. I understand why you might be pissed. I didn't come back to help you get off that ledge, but I'll bet you acquired lots of grit getting off by yourself." Don continued jabbering while drying by the fire. He was in one of his non-stop talking moods.

I fried some Spam in a skillet and made bush coffee. Don pulled out his hunting knife, speared a chunk of Spam from the skillet and sat it on a log to cool. He filled two metal cups with coffee and slid one toward me. "Are you planning to talk to me tonight or should I plan to talk to myself all night?"

"You're an idiot, Don. When I found out that you were alive and had not fallen to your death, I wanted to kill you myself. In fact, I'm still considering it. Hunting accidents take the lives of many careless hunters, you know."

We argued about the events of the past couple of days until the frost crept into camp. The black sky filled with frosty dots, and chilled me. I was emotionally and physically beat.

"You can stay up all night if you want, Don. I'm heading to bed." I started toward the tent.

"Dennis, I have a little problem. I lost my sleeping bag on the mountain. I couldn't get it into my pack with the goatskins, so I tied it to the top. It must have slipped off on my trip back."

"I guess you have a problem, Don. Your problem is not my problem." I crawled inside my bag and turned toward the tent wall, waiting for the rest my body needed.

Don crawled into the tent, lit the gas lamp, and settled down to read. "I see you didn't lose your paperback out there. Read it all night if you want. Maybe it will keep you warm."

He thumbed through the book, found a particular page, and then tore off the corner piece and popped it in his mouth. *This guy is weird.* I closed my eyes, leaving Don to his book.

The freezing cold woke me early the next morning. I realized that somehow Don had managed to unzip my sleeping bag and had spread it over both of us. He was sleeping comfortably, but I shivered with the cold. I got up, stirred the fire, and threw on some logs. Before long, the flames warmed me, first on the backside and finally to the core. *Jim might come back to pick us up today. I'll tidy the camp and get ready, just in case.*

I stripped naked and waded across the river to release the rope tied on the far side. After freeing it, I pulled myself back to the shore where the tent was pitched. I carefully coiled the ropes, placed them in the duffle, and threw them behind the tent, and there they were! Four goatskins lay on the sand, completely caped and totally intact. Don had placed a pair of horns above each cape, making it appear as if they were still attached to the bodies.

"Don, get out of bed. We need to talk." I waited for him to emerge from the tent, becoming angrier by the minute. He finally appeared and walked over to absorb the heat from my fire.

"I want to know what is going on here, Don. No more bullshit. Did you shoot those four goats?"

"Yep, and each is a fine trophy."

"The Fish and Game officer told me that you don't have a hunting license. I thought you had put poaching behind you."

"You have no idea what it's like to be hooked on something. I saw them and I shot them. It's my thing and it's none of your business."

"Now, tell me what's going on with the paperback. What's the deal with chewing on the corners of your book?"

He started to walk away, but he knew I wouldn't give up. "I have a friend in California who puts a drop of acid on the corner of every seventh page. You know, acid…LSD." He stared at me for a minute and then continued. "You don't know anything, do you? I love to get high. I can't stop. Sorry, that's just the way it is. Jean is a good Mormon, but I couldn't care less about that stuff."

Don took a couple of steps away from the tent and relieved himself. I saw the book beside the gas lamp, grabbed it and threw it into the fire. It was nearly consumed before he realized it was burning.

"What the hell! You just cost me several hundred dollars."

"I'm not spending my time out here with you stoned. I better not find any more drugs in this camp."

We exchanged only a few words for the remainder of that day. It was late afternoon when Jim landed in the middle of the lake to take us home.

"Don, gather your stuff and get out of here on the first flight. Take these poached goats with you. I don't want them in my camp."

Don waded out to the floatplane and made several trips carrying his gear to the plane. "Tell Jim to come back for me tomorrow. It'll be too dark to safely land here tonight."

Jim returned for me the following day. He flew my gear and me to Fire Lake at Eagle River. Carol met me with the pickup and helped load everything into the back. "Honey, something must be wrong with Don. He picked up all his tools and walked off the job. Did you two have a fight?"

"Don nearly killed me out there. I thought about killing him. Yeah, I'd say we have a fractured friendship."

Don was fined $750 for hunting without a license. Fish and Game never knew that he had poached four mountain goats on that hunt. We renewed our friendship over time. I chose to forget his carelessness that nearly cost me my life, and overlooked his drug use.

Don bought a Piper PA12 and during the next few years, we often flew together hunting and exploring the Alaskan bush. Considering Don demonstrated exceptional abilities in everything he attempted, I was not surprised that he became an accomplished pilot.

At about the same time, the California Wildlife Department, the IRS, and the drug lord from California tracked Don and discovered him in Alaska. One Sunday morning in March, Don came to talk to me in private. He was as serious as I'd ever seen him.

"Dennis, I'm going to die in the next few weeks. When they find my body, I will be gone forever, but don't mourn because it won't be me." He explained in detail how he planned to stage his death. When we said good-bye, he thanked me for our friendship, shook my hand, and then unexpectedly gave me a big hug. "I'll never see you again but I want to thank you for everything. You taught me more than all the others before you."

"Don, are you stoned again?"

"Not this time, Dennis."

Don followed through with his plan. Several weeks later, Don's plane failed to arrive in Kotezbue as scheduled. After a month of searching for him, Search and Rescue called off the search to find the missing airplane. Everyone believed that he had died.

Jean received a million dollar life insurance check and disappeared with her three children.

Don was the craziest friend I ever had. Someday, Ill tell you how he pulled off his biggest fraud. It's an amazing story, but that will have to wait until my next book.

Don, if you read this story, lift your glass in memory of all our experiences together.

Family Car

Alaska was discovered when the first Asians walked across the ice bridge close to the Arctic Circle near modern day Teller, Alaska. Millenniums later, wooden ships traveled costal waterways seeking wealth from the Great Land's sea. Men afoot, or with teams of dogs, trespassed the interior finding riches beyond imagination and an enormous landscape, indescribable in mere words. The rush for gold and good fortune brought thousands of people to Nome, Skagway, and other seaport communities. Few were able to explore the vast emptiness until the arrival of the airplane.

If Alaska were divided in two, Texas would become the third largest state in the union. With a land mass this size, and the keys to God's own vault, you would expect a modern Alaskan highway system of four lane roads leading everywhere. What you find are few roads and every available means of transportation possible. Everything that rolls, crawls, floats, or flies can be found in the North, but the king of travel is the aircraft. The Great Land wouldn't have been explored without it. There are more aircraft in Alaska than anywhere else on earth.

Willy, our land transportation, was a green Jeep of the mid 60's vintage, with a canvas top, a V6 engine, and a heater that worked well on warm days, and not at all on cold ones. One hundred thirty-six thousand miles aged Willy; ocean spray and salted streets invited cancer to eat away at his sides and fenders.

It was the first time in months that Willy ventured out of Talkeetna, since owning an airplane afforded me the privilege of flying to Anchorage or Wasilla for supplies. I wouldn't have taken Willy this time, but I needed a part for my plane and it couldn't fly without it. I had no choice but drive.

Carol noticed the first sign of trouble as we drove into Eagle River. "Honey, should we be making this much smoke?"

"That can't be coming from Willy, Carol. I don't see anything behind us."

Willy's engine had been puffing for a long time, but this was more smoke than usual. This was "mosquito fogger" smoke, maybe even "forest fire" smoke, thick, "hang-in-the-air" smoke.

"I don't like to give you bad news, Honey, but Willy is making the air blue."

"You love giving me bad news, Carol. You live for bad news."

"That's not true and you know it. You better be thinking of something fast because at the current smog rate, Willy is going to choke this highway to a stop."

Fortunately, there was a service station just ahead, so I pulled Willy up next to the office. The attendant came out and yelled, "You had better shut that thing off before you scare away all my customers."

"Sorry, I've no idea what's causing this thing to make so much smoke." I examined the engine and couldn't see any visible reason for the fog. When I checked the oil dipstick, the oil had fallen below the full mark.

"I can't remember if I checked the oil before we left Talkeetna, Carol. Willy is two quarts low."

"So, any ideas? We can't get this piece of junk home tonight if it keeps burning oil like this."

"Easy Lovie, Willy has feelings, too. He got us through the last three years. I know he's dying, but I think we can get the plane part and make it home in time to pick up the kids from school."

I purchased a case of oil, threw it in the back seat, and poured four quarts in the engine. "I put two extra quarts of oil in the engine, Carol. It's only about fifteen miles to Merrill Field. I think we can make it there before I have to add more oil."

"This is beginning to remind me of our trip up the Alcan Highway. If we have to stop and check the oil every fifteen miles, we may not get home for a day or two."

"Lovie, we'll get home just fine. Willy has heart."

When we arrived at Reeve Air Parts at Merrill Field, I ran in and purchased the part, then checked the oil again.

"This isn't good, Lovie. We've consumed all the oil in the engine crankcase."

"Dennis, now what are we going to do?"

"I'll over-fill the engine by two quarts and head for Eagle River. I'll check it again at the same station where we stopped earlier."

"I don't think that station attendant will be thrilled to see you."

"I'm not trying to be his friend. I just want to get home."

This time, I parked down the street a ways so as not to cause too much annoyance from my billowing Jeep. When I checked the oil level, I found only a dark dot on the dipstick.

"Carol, we've consumed twelve quarts of oil in the last thirty miles. At our present oil consumption rate, we will need about thirty-six quarts to get home."

"Are we burning the oil or just pumping it through the engine? If we were burning that much oil, it seems we'd have fouled spark plugs and a lot more trouble than just blue smoke."

"Dang, Lovie, you're pretty smart for an old bush gal. If we had thicker oil, it wouldn't be consumed as quickly. That gives me an idea."

A few minutes later, I toted a five-gallon pail of 90-weight gear lubrication across the parking lot of the service station.

"You've got to be kidding, Dennis. You'll ruin the engine if you try to use that heavy grease in the crankcase."

"Desperate times call for desperate measures, Honey. I'm afraid this is Willy's last trip home. His engine's gone; Willy is dying of old age and ugly disease."

We stopped several times on our way home to put gear grease in the engine crankcase. The thicker oil slowed the oil consumption some, but by the time we arrived Talkeetna, we were out of heavy gear lube. I stopped at the driveway that leads to the elementary school.

"Lovie, why don't you get the boys and take them home. I'll find a resting place for Willy and be home soon."

For years people had been parking derelict autos at the Talkeetna Railroad Station. I found a space between two rusted hulks and squeezed in the tired old Jeep. I gathered up all my personal effects and the plane part, and then walked home.

"What did you do with Willy, Dennis?"

"I left him at the retirement home, Lovie. We're down to one vehicle now and *it* flies."

Willy became the city home of a "bush" man, building a cabin near Chase. But when he was in Talkeetna, he chose Willy as his town dwelling. Willy rested among the other rusted road monuments and further decayed. At times, I stopped to gaze at the old Jeep, until someone removed all the Junkers from along the railroad tracks. Willy and the other road ornaments were gone for good.

In time we bought an old Ford pickup and later our first helicopter. Driving rubber tires on concrete highways is the last choice for aviators of the Alaskan bush. About once a month Carol and I flew to Wasilla for groceries, a flight of less than an hour.

After landing our Super Cub on the gravel runway near the tiny mall, we'd look for a parking space close to the exit, so we wouldn't have to push the cart so far. Often, other bush pilots took the best parking spots; then we had to push the grocery cart over gravel to the plane. After our carts were filled with necessities and a few "goodies," we faced the problem of loading all the stuff into our small plane. Carol knelt in the aft seat facing backwards, and I handed her items for storage in the baggage compartment.

"Dennis, start with the things that can't break or be crushed. That means no eggs! Pass me the dried beans, rice, and flour. The pancake mix and powered milk are next. The fruit and eggs go on top."

"Lovie, I don't want more than 120 pounds behind the seat. We have to keep the load balanced."

"There's not too much weight in the back. Let me get buckled in, and you can stack the rest around me."

"Good job, Carol. I'll try not to put too many heavy goods on your lap this time." With the groceries stacked nearly to the skylight, Carol hung onto them to keep them from falling into my space.

"Dennis, get this thing off the ground. I hate being packed in here like a sardine."

About an hour later, I taxied the Super Cub to the front of our house and parked next to my old pickup. I unpacked my "bird" under Carol's close scrutiny, since she didn't want to lose even one item from her precious cargo. Then we reversed the process; Everything categorized and placed carefully on the ground, then moved inside the house, where Carol knew exactly where each article belonged.

"Dennis, careful with those eggs. You broke most of a flat the last trip. I don't want to see even a cracked shell this time. Take the fruit in first. I don't want any of it damaged from the cold. Don't bruise it, either. That stuff is more precious than gold."

"You're probably right, Lovie. Lots of cabins here in this mining region have gold cached away, but I'll bet ours is the only one with a papaya."

Everyone in the bush agrees that the aircraft is the king of travel, every adult, that is. Our teenage sons often protested about being seen in our old

Ford pickup. After a flight to Anchorage to catch the latest movie, they were embarrassed about walking, or paying for a taxi ride to the theater.

"A Dodge Charger would be nice, Dad. A Corvette, even better. Well, I suppose we three boys couldn't fit in a Corvette. Then how about a Firebird, something with real muscle?"

I endured this juvenile assault daily, and not from just one boy. The three of them spoke with one voice.

"Guys, get real. We fly to town in less than an hour in the helicopter. Would you rather spend three to four hours traveling down a lonely highway to go to the movie?"

Cory fired back. "All our cousins in the lower 48 have cars. They get to take their girlfriends to the movie in a car, not a taxi."

"Son, it's only a short taxi ride from the airport to the movie house. Remember when we used to land in the theater parking lot? But one time someone called the cops, said the helicopter made too much noise. It's only a mile walk from Merrill Field. You boys can hoof it."

"Dad, please get us a decent car. We hate walking or being chauffeured around. It's not cool. What girl wants to go to the movie in a taxi?"

"Okay, boys. I've never given much thought as to what a teenage girl might like. I'll work on getting you boys a car."

On a cold March morning several months later, Dave made the decision to take down an old birch tree that threatened to fall on the hanger in the next strong wind. He picked up the chainsaw and walked outside to kill the tree. I heard the chainsaw's roar as it ripped into the doomed timber. Moments later, the noise came to an abrupt halt, and I heard what sounded like a mountain lion's scream.

I raced outside and around the corner to find Dave surrounded by a patch of red snow. The scalpel sharp saw blade had cut through several layers of artic clothing, exposing muscle and the white bone beneath.

"Dave, what happened? That looks real nasty."

"I guess I brushed my leg with the saw. How bad is it?"

"I can see all the way to China. We've got to stop the bleeding. Press my handkerchief on the wound to stop the blood flow. I'll get Carol. She'll know what to do. Don't you dare pass out, or I'll ground you, and you won't fly for a month."

Just then, Carol came around the side of the hangar. She quickly surveyed the gruesome scene, and in her usual collected manner, assessed the damage, snapping orders as she worked on Dave's injury.

"Dennis, I'll get the bleeding under control. You get the truck warmed up. This wound needs the attention of a doctor. We'll have to take him to Palmer Hospital."

We moved Dave to the office floor. I leaned over and whispered to Carol, "Honey, that leg looks like a butchered moose quarter."

She gave me a dirty look. "Dennis, get the truck around here and put a sock in it. Dave's scared to death already."

"I hate to give you more bad news, Lovie, but Ford isn't going to start in this cold. We have a warm helicopter in the hangar. It'll be ready to fly in a couple minutes."

In about an hour, I hovered to a landing near the front door of the Palmer Hospital with Dave and Carol onboard. The hospital staff was ready, and quickly transported him beyond the sliding glass doors. I secured the helicopter and walked inside, looking for Carol in the waiting room.

I heard Dave's screams and felt relieved to know he was very much alive. Soon the screaming ceased, and the normal hospital sounds resumed. An hour or so later, a young doctor appeared to give me an update on his patient's condition.

"The ragged wound needed lots of trimming before suturing." He proceeded to give more grisly details than I cared to hear.

Later, a heavily sedated Dave was delivered to the helicopter for the flight home. A week later he was back on his feet, ornery as ever. Though we teased him unmercifully about his screams, he never admitted it was his voice I heard crying out.

FAMILY CAR

"Carol, I think it's time to buy a car. If the weather had been real nasty, I don't think I could've flown Dave to the hospital. I guess the boys are right. We need a family car. I'll be back later tonight, or tomorrow."

I caught a ride with someone going to Anchorage and returned the next day with a brand new car.

"Dad, have you lost it? This is not a car! This is a station wagon. Nobody would take a girl on a date in a station wagon."

"Les, take it easy. Think about the possibilities. Now, you can take eight or nine friends to town. Besides, you're too young to date anyway. A friend that happens to be a girl is okay, but no girlfriends."

Grudging acceptance soon turned to satisfaction. One Saturday morning the new Plymouth station wagon disappeared down Talkeetna Spur Road fully loaded with the boys' classmates. Television wasn't yet available in Talkeetna, so the rowdy group got off to an early start; they could take in three or four movies before returning home after midnight. They drove away with only a few murmurs of "Thunderbird, GTO, or Mustang."

By this time our business had expanded to include a six-passenger Cessna 206. Occasionally, I allowed the boys to fly it to Merrill Field to see a movie. Parents who live in the "lower 48" would never allow their children this luxury, but for Alaskan bush families, flying is part of adolescent development. The boys didn't consider flying to town a special treat. They often elected to drive the station wagon. At times they even petitioned me to sell the Cessna and buy them a sports car. I reminded them that a sports car didn't provide many prospects for generating revenue, so the Cessna remained.

Late one snow swept night the family car hadn't returned from Anchorage on time. After an hour or so of worrying, the phone rang. It was the dreaded ring that every parent fears, the one that brings bad news.

"Mr. Brown, this is Officer Van Gilder with the Alaska State Troopers. Your station wagon with nine juveniles on board struck a moose. The moose had to be put down."

"Officer, I'm real sad about the moose, but what about the kids?"

"Well, the front of the car is demolished, and the windshield caved in when the moose struck it. The kids were covered with broken glass and a few scratches. They're shaken up, but no one needs medical attention."

"Thank God! I appreciate you calling. What do you want me to do?"

"It's 30 below out here, and the kids need to get out of this cold. I doubt we could get a wrecker to come out this late, and there's no place to park the car on the roadway with the snow berms so high. It's only forty miles to Talkeetna, so the kids should be able to see through the broken windshield and limp it home ok."

"Could you follow them home? And tell them to take it slow and be extra careful."

"Sorry, I can't see them home. My shift ended over an hour ago. I still have a long drive to Houston."

It was well past midnight when the wreck pulled into our yard.

"I'm so glad you kids made it home safe. What happened?"

"We were being careful, Dad. We were only going 55 mph when a moose bounded over the snow berm and we plowed into it. The impact threw it over the car and into the bush. It was suffering, so Dave shot it in the head with the revolver."

"Cory, what revolver?'

"The one in the glove box."

"Oh, that one. Guess I forgot it was there. What did the trooper say about that?"

"He was glad Dave put it out of its misery. He was a little squeamish, shot at it three times and missed, but Dave finished it with one shot."

The trauma of that night diminished with time. The Cessna 206 became the boys' primary mode of transportation. They didn't want to be seen traveling in a taxi, so they chose to trek across town to the movie. After each action movie, there were more requests for the latest muscle car, but they were rejected. The chance of the boys hitting a flying moose was miniscule.

A faint light retreated from the sky as the plane departed from Talkeetna for another movie night at the Fireweed Theater. Light snow moved in during the early evening, and now the boys were overdue.

"Dennis, the boys should have been back over an hour ago. I'm worried."

"There's no one I can call at this hour, Lovie. There're no lighted runways between here and Anchorage. All we can do is wait and pray."

Waiting for news of your children makes a moment in time feel like forever. The ring of the phone broke through our worry, but we dreaded answering it. If the boys had been delayed for weather they would have called earlier.

"Mr. Brown?"

"Yes."

"This is Officer Dugan of the Anchorage Police Department. I have some bad news for you."

"What's happened?"

Carol watched me intently with tears welling up.

"I was on patrol this evening when I observed three juveniles climb over the security fence at Merrill field and walk over to your plane. I watched them enter the plane and attempt to start the engine. At that point, I shined my flashlight on them and summoned them to get out of your airplane. I took them into custody and plan to book them for attempted theft."

"You're kidding!"

"No, Sir. I'm not. They claim to have your permission to fly the plane, but I know that can't be true. They're too young to be pilots."

"Officer, are those juveniles wearing black leather jackets and carrying large hunting knives?"

"Yes, sir. You're correct about the leather jackets, and each is armed."

"Officer Dugan, those boys are my sons. Their mother is worried sick about them. Could you return them to the plane, and send them home immediately."

"It's not possible! They're only kids."

"They're my kids, officer. They fly that plane to Anchorage every week to see a movie. They're licensed pilots, and I want them home now."

"For heaven's sake, Mr. Brown. I'd never had guessed. Would you consider adopting me?"

"No chance of that, but I thank you for getting them on their way."

About an hour later, we heard the whine of the turbo-powered engine, and then the scatter of gravel as the plane landed on the runway. Carol and I regained our composure before the boys walked in the front door.

"Well, boys. What do you three have to say for yourselves?"

Les, the youngest answered. "Well, Dad. We will never take the short cut over the fence at Merrill Field again. From now on we'll walk down the road. We promise." Cory nodded in agreement.

I tried to look real stern. "Cory, I think you might be right. You boys need a car of your own, so you can drive to Anchorage."

"Thanks, Dad, but from now on, our family car is that Cessna 206. Only in Alaska can a teenager fly to the movies. We're the luckiest kids around. It's so cool!"

"You finally get it, Cory. In Alaska, the family car is a Cessna."